HEMINGWAY
AT
EIGHTEEN

HEMINGWAY
AT
EIGHTEEN

The Pivotal Year
That Launched
an American Legend

STEVE PAUL

CHICAGO
REVIEW
PRESS

To my late parents,
Bill and Barbara Steinhardt, who always believed.

Copyright © 2018 by Steve Paul
Foreword copyright © 2018 by Paul Hendrickson
All rights reserved
First edition
Published by Chicago Review Press Incorporated
814 North Franklin Street
Chicago, Illinois 60610
ISBN 978-1-61373-971-6

Library of Congress Cataloging-in-Publication Data
Names: Paul, Steve, 1953– author.
Title: Hemingway at eighteen : the pivotal year that launched an American
  legend / Steve Paul.
Description: First edition. | Chicago, Illinois : Chicago Review Press, 2017.
  | Includes bibliographical references and index.
Identifiers: LCCN 2017007515 (print) | LCCN 2017009157 (ebook) | ISBN
  9781613739716 (cloth) | ISBN 9781613739723 (adobe pdf) | ISBN
  9781613739747 (epub) | ISBN 9781613739730 (kindle)
Subjects: LCSH: Hemingway, Ernest, 1899–1961—Childhood and youth. | Authors,
  American—20th century—Biography.
Classification: LCC PS3515.E37 Z7525 2017 (print) | LCC PS3515.E37 (ebook) |
  DDC 813/.52 [B] —dc23
LC record available at https://lccn.loc.gov/2017007515

Typesetting: Nord Compo

Printed in the United States of America
5 4 3 2 1

CONTENTS

FOREWORD

Ernest Hemingway was born five months in front of the twentieth century, on July 21, 1899. Among other things, this makes keeping mental track of his age a relatively easy task. For instance: we know without needing to think about it that Pearl Harbor happened on December 7, 1941—thus, Hemingway must have been forty-two. The Wright brothers flew at Kitty Hawk in December 1903, ergo a sturdy little incipient genius in Oak Park in his short pants had to have been nearly five months past his fourth birthday. (Come to think, maybe he was in woolen knickers that day—it was the onset of an Illinois winter.) JFK in Dealey Plaza? If Hemingway were alive (he was two years dead), he would have been sixty-four. This instant calculating tool or clocking device or whatever you wish to call it works just as effortlessly for events in the author's own life. If you know when *The Sun Also Rises* came out (fall of 1926), then you automatically know he was twenty-seven. Since I am a person challenged by math, it occurs to me to say that, along with all the gifts Hemingway left us, for all time, he slyly slid under the door jamb this one: puny, and not puny at all.

It occurs to me to say that the sly gift Steve Paul has given us in *Hemingway at Eighteen* is an idea that has been hiding in plain sight for a long time. He takes us into one extraordinary year in an extraordinary life—namely, from July 21, 1917, to July 21,

1918—and has the cheek to try to make the part stand for the whole. In his introduction he allows that his project is essentially presumptuous, the notion that any biographer might find, like a pearl resting inside a shell, "the whole of the man in a single, twelve-month grain of sand." I agree: such a thing isn't quite possible. It is a bit presumptuous. A synecdoche is finally a synecdoche. But you can come damn close, and, in fact, Paul does. In this short, pointed work, which doesn't attempt to oversell itself, I have learned nearly as much about Hemingway—or at least gotten a visceral feel for the young Ernest Hemingway—as I have from works twice or three times this size. In the bargain, as I read, I was getting a good visceral feel for the young twentieth century itself. In full, as we know, it was a century of blood and grief, of mass slaughters the world hadn't previously conjured, even as it was a century of stupendous (and not-conjured) technological and scientific breakthrough. It was a century of art and literature, too. It was as if the century at seventeen going on eighteen, no less than the boy-man at eighteen, was foreshadowing all that each would separately be.

It is a fool's errand—which Paul doesn't run—to bother oneself with the question of: What was *the* most critical year in Hemingway's life? That's like asking: What was the single most important year of the twentieth century? Leave it at this: the period of 1917–1918, for both America and Hemingway, was hugely important. For both century and man, there was an exit from the garden, a kind of going from innocence to sin, from shelter to what Bob Dylan might call "no direction home." For Hemingway, the going, in the early part of his eighteenth-ness, was from the protections of suburban Oak Park and the big family house on Kenilworth Avenue (never mind that there was doom lurking inside that house) to the wide-open grit and protofrontier joys of Kansas City. It was his first real job, and it was on a great American newspaper. It is reductionist and oversimplifying the matter to say that Hemingway learned to write in those six and a half months that he spent as a cub at the *Kansas City Star*. Reductionist and oversimplifying, OK, but unarguable, too, that the *Star* taught him things about the power of short, declarative, linear, action-based *American* sentences. Such sentences became the brick and mortar of the uncopy-able Hemingway style. (You can parody the Hemingway style, but you can't begin to copy it.)

Steve Paul, who spent a long, honorable career at the *Star*, in what he unashamedly thinks of as "the brotherhood" of the *Star*, and who is now recently retired from his inky labors there (though I doubt retired from the brotherhood aspects), is superbly qualified to tell us this tale.

The second part of the year of eighteenth-ness, as every Hemingway student knows, has to do with the war in Europe. He left Missouri and went into the still-wider world, where there was nothing *proto* about the violence. He entered the ambulance service of the American Red Cross and, two weeks before his nineteenth birthday, was blown up—spiritually more than physically, but physically all the same—on the iconic banks of the Piave River. Well, if the banks weren't iconic then, they were destined to be, through the myth of his life, the myth of his writing. It is equally reductionist and oversimplifying to say that what happened on the front in Italy gave Hemingway the material he needed to become an immortal figure in our literature. But at the same time it is unarguable that that experience, terrible as it was, was the brick and mortar (in two senses of the word *mortar*) of some beautiful edifices to come.

The Kansas City days and the World War I days were brief things for Ernest Hemingway. It didn't matter. As he told us in another place, it is never the duration of an experience but rather the intensity of an experience that matters. If you feel it authentically enough, the sensation will last you a lifetime. And us, too.

—Paul Hendrickson, October 2016

Paul Hendrickson is the author of *Hemingway's Boat* (2011), which primarily traces the last thirty years of Ernest Hemingway's life. After a long career as a staff writer at the *Washington Post*, he joined the creative writing faculty at the University of Pennsylvania. A previous book, *Sons of Mississippi*, won the National Book Critics Circle Award in general nonfiction.

INTRODUCTION

Oh Boy. Oh Man. Oh Hemingstein.
—ERNEST HEMINGWAY TO HIS SISTER MARCELLINE

Forgive me, Nadine Gordimer, for I have ignored something I heard you say years ago about Ernest Hemingway. "Let us leave his life alone," you told an audience in Boston, where we had gathered to take note of the writer's one hundredth birthday anniversary. "It belongs to him. Let's read his books. His gift to us belongs to us all." So, yes, the book at hand is, indeed, about Hemingway's life though not at all divorced from his work.

Hemingway is quite likely the American author of the twentieth century who has been the most argued about, dissected, and puzzled over to this day. His life grew to mythic proportions. His work, or much of it, remains canonical, inspiring, mysterious, and powerfully, surprisingly relevant to humans with a heart in a world shaped by war and anxiety. Popular culture retains him as a complicated force of nature. Books by and about him continue to make waves and news.

My biographical project to examine Hemingway's early adulthood, or late teenhood, began nearly two decades ago, just a few months before that centennial conference, in April 1999, at the John F. Kennedy Presidential Library in Boston. Like Hemingway, my newspaper work first appeared in the *Kansas City Star* when I was eighteen years old. Very much unlike Hemingway, who made a point of getting out of newspapering before it ruined him, I stuck around. Others can speculate on the ruin brought about by my life choice.

This book does not examine the entirety of Hemingway's life. It barely brushes his earliest years in Oak Park, Illinois, and northern Michigan. It ends long before the creative peaks and valleys of Hemingway's last two decades in Cuba, before the two plane crashes in Africa, before the sad and troubling decline into irredeemable depression and the cold and brutal finality of his suicide.

Its emphasis on a single year of the Hemingway journey is admittedly a presumptuous slice of biography, an attempt to find the whole of the man in a single, twelve-month grain of sand. But what a year it was. This was the year that Hemingway's life of self-invention began. His path toward writing as a viable career began in the fertile newsroom of a great American newspaper. It wound precipitously but eternally through a near-death experience in a wartime trench in Italy.

To be an eighteen-year-old in America undoubtedly has evolved since Hemingway's time. A much smaller percentage of young Americans went to college in those days than is the case today, so Hemingway's decision to work instead was not all that unusual. What was unusual was that, at eighteen, he began to shape a vision of his own future in a powerful and resonant way. That future, as we know, took on an epic level of fame and celebrity that remains rare, especially for those who labor to put words on paper yet manage to connect with millions of readers around the globe.

Hemingway's apprenticeship in journalism, his first six-and-a-half-month stint as a reporter in Kansas City, is generally acknowledged, at least in passing, as having been constructive. (At least one recent Hemingway biographer, however, didn't find the need to even mention it.) No biographer or critic has spent fruitful, quality time examining that period deeply since the Yale scholar Charles A. Fenton in the early 1950s. This book aims to bring new detail and new perspective on Hemingway's *Kansas City Star* experience. Hemingway would be horrified by the presentation in these pages of some of his newspaper work, the un-bylined juvenilia that he wished were lost to history. That writing, he said, had nothing to do with his "real" writing, which he began in Paris just four years after leaving Kansas City. But then again, some of that early experience did indeed emerge in his writing consciousness in the 1920s.

Beyond the Kansas City apprenticeship, Hemingway was still eighteen when he signed up for the American Red Cross ambulance service in Italy, crossed the ocean to Europe, and, two weeks before his nineteenth birthday, somehow withstood the biting assault of an exploding mortar shell at a post along the battered banks of the Piave River. Many young men go to war, and if they survive, they return home scarred in ways we do not always understand. Hemingway was a noncombatant in the Great War, but his wounding was real and long lasting. The physical wounds would soon be compounded by emotional ones, ever deepening the wellspring that led to all the greater Hemingway themes of love, loss, betrayal, endurance, brokenness, morality, and the specter of death.

No matter how we feel about the supposedly macho, sloppy man, serial husband, and great American writer of the twentieth century, Susan Beegel has reminded us that, in his work, "we learn something about ourselves." The themes and subjects of his stories and novels often seem eerily up to date. They explore the full range of human values, the moral consequences of our decision making, and boundless stretches of territory, from his beloved Michigan pine barrens, scarred by industrialization, to the crime-haunted streets of Kansas City, the gossipy sidewalk cafes of Paris, and the languid canals of Venice. And his writing opens a window into a place of deep understanding. In Hemingway, Beegel said at another centennial event that year, we learn that "seeing clear is the first step to saving the world."

In this immensely important formative period of his, as the Western world endured a war in 1917–18, the eighteen-year-old Hemingway began the process of seeing clear. He embraced a way of being that allowed him to demonstrate "how to live with exactitude and joy," as H. R. Stoneback has put it. Not all of it was joyful, of course. Hemingway's "launch year," the beginning of his life of independence and self-creation, opened his eyes and opened up the world for the taking.

A Note on Sources

Some of this account is based on Hemingway's correspondence, in which the writer was often at his loosest. His letters are sometimes perfunctory, sometimes untrustworthy, often improvisational and playful. Where direct quotes appear, I follow the editorial decisions made by the editors of the great current project to publish and annotate all six thousand plus of his known letters—four volumes released by Cambridge University Press as of fall 2017—complete with Hemingway's errors of spelling, syntax, and punctuation intact.

PROLOGUE

I wanted to write about the whole damned world
if I could get to know it.
—Ernest Hemingway

He was a hero now. A superstar. And with his graying brush of a mustache and his new honey-haired bride alongside, he cut a swaggering figure as he paced the hotel room to chat. Sure, an interview for old time's sake would be swell. It would be fun to reminisce. A break from the grinding drive.

It was a Monday in November 1940, cool and wet with rain, when Ernest Hemingway and Martha Gellhorn arrived in Kansas City for the night. They'd motored in from Wyoming. They had been married in Cheyenne four days earlier. They planned to catch a train to New York, boarding at the vast, bustling Union Station, which Ernest knew so well from his days as a beginning newspaper reporter more than twenty years in the past. "The 'Cub' Comes Back with a Bride," is how the paper put it the next morning. Hemingway's return "to His First Field" was front-page news in Kansas City. Just a few weeks earlier, Scribner's had published Hemingway's big new novel of the Spanish Civil War. So the author, who had witnessed one war as a teenaged noncombatant in the Red Cross ambulance service and covered others as a journalist, was ready for adulation, and he was happy to toast the old haunts in this midwestern American city.

Four days after their wedding in Wyoming, Ernest Hemingway and Martha Gellhorn traveled through Kansas City and paused for an interview with a reporter from his old paper. *Ernest Hemingway Collection, John F. Kennedy Presidential Library, Boston. Used with permission of the* Kansas City Star

Hemingway wore boots, a plaid tie, and a casual tweed jacket with the cuffs folded up. Rain peppered the window. He picked through his memories of Kansas City and shared them with Paul Fisher, a reporter for the *Star*'s morning edition, who was assigned to meet up with the famous writer. Hemingway stood in his room at the Muehlebach Hotel, the downtown landmark whose dark halls he'd walked twenty-two years earlier. In his day here, the hotel pressroom had given Hemingway a place to work and relax out of sight from his bosses at the *Star*'s building eight blocks away. He wrote letters back home on Muehlebach stationery. He told Fisher you could sleep in the bathtub "if your knees articulated properly." After a long day and night chasing stories, that uncomfortable shut-eye was more convenient than taking the streetcar home. A few years after this visit, Hemingway would remember the Muehlebach and place it in the dreams of his melancholy colonel, Richard Cantwell, in *Across the River and into the Trees*. The hotel "has the biggest beds in the world," Cantwell says to the young countess, "and we'll pretend that we are oil millionaires."

But now Hemingway remembered the Kansas City of his youth, the brief, formative apprenticeship he served on the way to seeing the Great War in Italy and becoming a writer. What a time it was. There was a shoot-out between detectives and internal revenue agents, and Hemingway crawled under a car as the bullets flew. An oddball case of mistaken identity among lawmen—that was a good story, good enough that Fisher folded a memory of it into his opening paragraph. That was the Hemingway people expected: a man who talked big and brash, a man who knew how violence molds the world and shapes people, a man, indeed, who was shaped by violence and the trauma of war. When William M. Reddig, the *Star*'s book critic, reviewed *For Whom the Bell Tolls* a month before this visit, he said of Hemingway, "He still is the great chronicler of violence and death, the one novelist who most accurately and dramatically portrays the foremost phenomenon of our time."

For Hemingway, Kansas City was a transitional place, a stopping point between suburban youth and that traumatic, life-defining war. But also, for him, it was a place that made violence real. It took whatever boyhood education he had accumulated in the northern woods and gave it adult sinew and bone. The newspaper work brought him close to violence almost every day: knifings and street crime, grit and desperation, the kinds of urban eruptions that gave Kansas City a Wild West reputation, even two decades into the twentieth century.

Of all the places that shaped the life and myth of Ernest Hemingway—think of suburban Chicago, northern Michigan, Paris, Spain, Africa's safari lands, Key West, Cuba—Kansas City is the least romantic and most unknown. Hemingway came to know it as a place where eighteen-year-old boys became men. By day it was buttoned up, civic minded, bustling with church conventions and war bond luncheons. After dark it offered a different side. The young Hemingway, tall, gangly, and boyish faced, reveled in what he found there. He learned, for better or worse, from sage and wild journalists, from late-night hospital surgeons and ambulance drivers, from lawmen and jaded drunks. The heartland city gave substance to an idea that he would put to use just a few years later: "It is awfully easy to be hard-boiled about everything in the daytime, but at night it is another thing."

The eighteen-year-old Hemingway transformed himself in Kansas City. For one thing, the city prepared him, whether he realized it or not, for his journey to the war in Europe. In Italy, in the months after Kansas City, his life would change profoundly, too. And whatever latent notions Hemingway held about the war, personal duty, and the world, Kansas City helped alter and amplify them. As one of his closest friends once put it, Kansas City changed Hemingway from a "modest, rather shy and diffident boy" to a young man who was "aggressive and opinionated." Moreover, this boy in Kansas City became "an apostle of the violent." He was partial to fisticuffs and sided with dark angels. To this Hemingway, Kansas City showed itself as a place of cops and robbers, of graft and hypocrisy, of exotic tastes and temptations. It shaped the wounded outlook of Jake Barnes in *The Sun Also Rises*. It was a symbolic refuge for Harold Krebs, the shattered veteran who reads the Kansas City newspaper while his mother nags. It housed the jangly habits of a desperate burlesque-show loser in one of Hemingway's lesser-known stories, "A Pursuit Race." Shortly after Hemingway left Kansas City, in May 1918, bound for the ambulance service in Italy, a newspaper colleague wrote to him and urged him to put his special gift to work as he went to the war. Already, still just eighteen, Hemingway had made a lasting impression.

Now here, twenty-two years later in the Muehlebach Hotel, Kansas City seemed to mean something special, something quite personal to this outsized American celebrity. Fisher undoubtedly told Hemingway of the praise that Reddig, the book critic, had heaped on him in his review of *For Whom the Bell Tolls*: "Never before has he written so thoughtfully of man's courage, man's hope, man's unquenchable spirit in the hour of defeat." In his story for the next morning's paper, Fisher generously noted that the novel was "generally regarded as one of the best books any American ever has produced." Hemingway told Fisher how much effort it took these last two years and how pleased he was that Gary Cooper would star as Robert Jordan in Hollywood's version of the Spanish war tale. Cooper already had turned another Hemingway hero into cinematic reality, playing the love-struck ambulance driver Frederic Henry in *A Farewell to Arms*, a role that hinted at the lanky shyness of Hemingway in his wounded youth. But writing the novels was where the action was. "God knows I worked hard," Hemingway said of *For Whom the Bell Tolls*. "I put everything I had seen and known of the Spanish conflict in it as truly and as cleanly as I could."

Hemingway had to be polite to his visitor from the *Star*. It was a brotherhood to be a *Star* man, and though he had long been gone from that life, had washed newspaper writing from his system, Hemingway understood the role. So he had to meet expectations as the great writer who had gotten his training in this middle American town. Maybe he volunteered to Fisher what he thought *Star* men wanted to hear. Maybe Fisher teased it out of him. But certainly Hemingway retained a warm feeling for the Italianate brick fortress at Eighteenth and Grand. It was, after all, the place that gave him his professional start as a writer. So he recalled how his editors fostered good writing and, with their news-writing style sheet, instilled in him the tenets, as Fisher put it, of "clarity, conciseness and accuracy." The fabled style sheet—it's often remembered for its staccato beginning: "Use short sentences. Use short first paragraphs. Use vigorous English. Be positive, not negative." There were a hundred more entries about usage and grammar. "Those were the best rules I ever learned for the business of writing," Hemingway told Fisher. "I've never forgotten them. No man with any talent, who feels and writes truly about the thing he is trying to say, can fail to write well if he abides with them."

To be topical, the reporter picked Hemingway's brain about Europe's new war, or, more likely, he listened as Hemingway opined on the dark forces of fascism that were splitting the continent. Hemingway, the wounded young man of the first war and not long removed from the bullets and the bloodshed of the Spanish front, had opinions about all of it. He'd been eighteen back then in Kansas City and just beginning to truly comprehend the world, but now, at forty-one, he had seen, experienced, and come to understand so much more. "There is hardly an Italian home where death has not come from war in the last seven or eight years," Hemingway said, sounding more like speechifying than casual conversation. "Italy lost many men in Spain. The Loyalists could have won that war and this war would not have come had there been any decency from democratic countries in acknowledging merely in supplies the fight against fascism or egoism, such as Mussolini's or Hitler's egoism. Right was on the Loyalist side, and I still believe right, with other factors equal, usually wins."

Gellhorn was hungry. As her husband talked on about war she phoned for room service.

"You go ahead," Hemingway told her. "A woman should always eat when she is hungry. I'll wait for Luis and his wife."

The interview was about to take on the feel of a boisterous party. A friend from Spain, the exiled artist Luis Quintanilla, was dropping by to say hello. The former antifascist fighter was spending a year in Kansas City as artist in residence at the local university. He was painting frescoes for one of the campus buildings, scenes of Don Quixote and Sancho Panza in the modern world. Hemingway made sure there'd be time to visit with Luis, his wife, and their ten-month-old baby, and time, too, to hoist some cocktails and put on *la gran borrechera*, the great drunk, which had been their usual activity.

"*Cambiamos*," Ernest said as Luis's wife, Jan, came in the door. "Let's trade." And Ernest planted a kiss on Mrs. Quintanilla, a kiss she did not soon forget. Hemingway's brand-new wife watched but soon embraced Jan, too, as if they were old friends. Hemingway, with Spanish and English mixing in the air, roughhoused with Quintanilla and caught him in a crotch hold. The artist handed the newlyweds a gift: two sketches he'd made for the mural under way. Ernest loved the way Quintanilla sketched, admired the clean, direct style. He once wrote that he aspired to write the way that his artist friend drew.

A cartoon by the Spanish painter, Luis Quintanilla, of Ernest Hemingway, who has written the complete story of bullfighting in his new book, "Death in the Afternoon" (Scribners).

(*For release in the morning papers of September 23.*)

Luis Quintanilla's sketch of Hemingway as a torero *was distributed as a publicity piece for* Death In the Afternoon *in 1932. Rare Books and Special Collections, Firestone Library, Princeton University, Princeton, New Jersey. Used with permission*

At least one *Star* man remembered joining Hemingway and others at a tavern near the paper on the night of this visit. Others recalled Hemingway visiting the newsroom as well.

The *Star*'s Fisher could hardly have known much about the lives of Hemingway and his new bride. But he knew how to end a story with a memorable kicker. He noted that Martha Gellhorn had to report for duty in New York on December 7. Her magazine, *Collier's*, was going to send her to Europe on assignment, although she did not yet know where. "At any event," she told Fisher, "right now I'm the war correspondent in the family." It was a playful jab but still a stinging, competitive moment. In hindsight, of course, Gellhorn's quip hinted at the couple's relationship troubles to come.

If Ernest noticed, we do not know. But his mood that night was upbeat and playful, too. And here he was, the apostle of the violent, performing for a *Star* man and feeling as if he were in a place where he belonged. Two of Hemingway's boys were born in Kansas City. He still had a cousin here whose company he enjoyed. By now he'd broken most bonds with his mother in Chicago and his siblings elsewhere, so holding on to the good places made sense. Brummy and Odgar. Hopkins. Tubby. All of those strong connections he had formed in Kansas City. All those men who shaped and shared his experience, who'd helped lead him to his first adventure in Europe. And the *Star*. It all felt so real. Talking to Fisher brought a lot of it back. He could see it all again in his mind. Those wintry days. Those six months of growing up. Yes, he could see it. Walking his beat back then on a cold and damp day. This was how it was: in search of stories to tell, he could look up and see the hospital on the Kansas City hill rising out of the fog.

1

SUMMER OF INDECISION

You know you are much better fitted to be a newspaper man than anything else.
—Lucille Dick to Ernest Hemingway

The potato beds at Longfield Farm were parched. From the other side of the lake, Ernest Hemingway could stand in the perforated tree-shade near the family cottage and peer over toward the brown dirt he'd been working so hard that summer. His hands were toughened by hay cutting and shed building, and that part of it was done now. It was surprisingly cool for early August but dry enough to worry that the potatoes and the beans were in trouble. The fish were running good, though. A few nights earlier, after a long day in the field, he'd pulled some big rainbows and a two-pound brook trout out of the water near Horton Bay. And as he did often that summer while fishing the cool Michigan water and toiling in the summer fields, he churned the options in his mind. This, he knew, would be his last boyhood summer. Yet it was still unclear how his adult life would unfold.

His graduation from Oak Park and River Forest High School in June, five weeks before his eighteenth birthday, led straight to uncertainty. Many of Hemingway's friends in Oak Park would be off to the University of Illinois. His yearbook picture caption announced the same regarding his intentions, though Cornell and Princeton had also become tempting. His sister Marcelline was bound for Oberlin. And Hemingway, too, might have gone to that liberal Ohio school, because it was a family tradition. But college disappeared from his plans that year. Perhaps family finances were stretched too far to accommodate both Marcelline and Ernest in college. Or so went the rumors, according to one classmate: "We all thought it was unfair, as we kids felt that he should have had prior right." Still, Dr. Clarence Hemingway's small-town medical practice went only so far, especially with six children and an ambitious wife in the house. One thing Grace Hemingway wanted was her own cabin at the lake, a quiet place away from the family's Windemere cottage, a place where she could sing and perhaps paint, and that would come in due time.

Marcelline was a year older than her brother; she had been held back in grade school to concentrate on music, and thus she and her brother left high school at the same time. So if only one of them could go to college first, she had an advantage. But most likely, Marcelline was more determined than Ernest to advance to Oberlin. For her brother, college did not seem all that necessary. He liked to find things out for himself. Hemingway, perceived as the class "prophet," could exude a certain self-confidence, bolstered by his strapping good looks. The United States had just entered the war in Europe, and the idea of serving in the military also set in. But he placed that aside for a while, mostly discouraged by his father, who insisted he was too young. Nevertheless Hemingway already had built his own arsenal of interests. He had already absorbed the wisdom of his elders in the books and in the writing he'd explored in high school. He'd read Shakespeare. He'd kept detailed diaries. He'd written short stories. He'd chronicled excursions in the woods and on the Des Plaines River near his home. Sure, he might eventually get to the state university, possibly the following year, but first he wanted to get some work and life away from home under his belt.

As usual, the family had headed up from Oak Park for another summer season in the north country near Michigan's Little Traverse Bay. This year, for the first time, Clarence had a horseless carriage, a Model T Ford. The girls had gone with an aunt up Lake Michigan on the Manitou steamer, but Clarence drove Ernest, his wife, and the youngest, Leicester, on a five-day journey from their home. It was a road trip not without incident—a blown tire and other mechanical setbacks slowed them down. But they'd had a jolly gathering with relatives on the way and arrived at the cottage on Walloon Lake no worse for the wear.

Hemingway, now almost six feet tall, asserted his independence by pitching a tent outside, across the lake on the family's Longfield Farm acreage. Though his summer was not spent in total isolation from his family, it might as well have been. He was stubborn, combative, and intent on doing things his way. Oak Park, Illinois, where the Hemingways lived in a comfortable Victorian home, was a place where "citizens took pride in the past and distrusted the future, especially the new liberties and wild music favored by the younger generation." Hemingway was certainly interested in the liberties. He was clever, funny, somewhat unkempt—all uncharacteristic of the straitlaced Oak Parkers. And he kept his parents at arm's length and beyond. Dr. Hemingway was "a very arbitrary, very gruff man," said one of Hemingway's old friends. "He and Ernest did not get along then or at any time and I think home was none too attractive to Ernest."

In one way it seems ironic that Ernest and his mother didn't get along either. Grace Hall Hemingway, a woman devoted to life's creative pursuits, demanded that people have spunk and stand up. Most people thought of her as domineering. "My mother had little tolerance for people who had no gumption," Hemingway's younger sister Carol Hemingway Gardner recalled late in her life, adding that *gumption* was one of her mother's favorite words. "She herself was full of ideas and the will to carry them out. She was not interested in pale people who lamented their fate or who had no plans for the future." Hemingway may have dithered about his future in that summer of 1917, but he was hardly of the pale variety. Yet he mostly disappointed his mother with his youthful rambunctiousness and disregard for decorum. His feelings seemed to seethe under the surface one August day when he wrote to her, "Please don't burn any papers in my room or throw away anything that you don't like the looks of." Oh, the anxieties of youth.

Hemingway soon left his tent and boarded in town, in Horton Bay, about six miles west of Windemere, on Lake Charlevoix. The village, once home to a lumber mill, gave the sometimes awkward boy a chance to expand his social horizons. Liz and Jim Dilworth ran the Pinehurst Inn at Horton Bay and had become summer friends of the family. Hemingway referred to Liz as Aunt Beth and favored her cooking. Jim Dilworth ran a blacksmith shop. One night in June, Hemingway visited his friends Bill and Kate Smith at their aunt's place on Pincherry Road, a short stroll from the center of the village. Also visiting that night was a friend of the Smiths, J. Charles Edgar. Known as Carl and casually as Odgar, he had a thing for Kate. ("Odgar always wanted to marry Kate," Hemingway would later write.) Edgar was twenty-eight, but he and Hemingway hit it off in the few weeks they spent together. They fished often, until Edgar returned to Kansas City, where he was living and working.

If Hemingway had not yet begun considering a newspaper job there, Carl Edgar at least gave the young man an appealing reason to relocate and explore life elsewhere. Maybe he could go to

Kansas City to "seek his fortune." Hemingway told Edgar he'd show up and look for a job. Edgar undoubtedly served as an adult role model, a substitute father figure, a man of strong fiber who was anchored with a good job in the oil business. Odgar, Hemingway would write in one of his Nick Adams stories, "had been nicer to Nick than anybody ever had." He could be a good influence in Kansas City, a guide as the teenaged Hemingway left the nest and began to find his own way in the world. Still, at the beginning of the summer of 1917 Hemingway was hardly thinking about a career of any kind. Hemingway then was as "ingenuous a youth as I have ever met," Edgar later wrote, "large and handsome with no thought but fishing and the outdoors in general."

Hemingway's letters over the summer revealed his struggle to make a decision about his future. At one time he thought he'd become a doctor. Now he wasn't so sure. To one relative he said he'd either go live with an uncle in California or try to get a job at the *Chicago Tribune*. If he went to his uncle Leicester's, he'd save up money for school in a year. This would be the University of Illinois option—to California first, then back on the college track. Another uncle promoted the idea of newspaper work. Tyler Hemingway had told Ernest he could get him a summer job at the *Kansas City Star*, a towering newspaper based in the heart of the country and distributed in seven states. Then it turned out the *Star* could not take the boy on until fall. So if that appealed to him, Hemingway could wait it out up in Michigan, explore the lake and the woods, and consider other options in his budding exercise at self-creation.

For a while, he might have led his parents and uncle on by saying he'd take that Kansas City job. Later in the summer, his high school English teacher, Fannie Biggs, tried to line up interviews for Hemingway at two of the Chicago papers. But eventually he figured the summer work on the farm was his main laboring effort for the time. Later he suggested he might work in Jim Dilworth's blacksmith shop, at least through October. And fishing certainly filled out many of his summer days.

In previous summers Ernest had imagined a life as an explorer or following his interest in the natural sciences. His father had taught him about the outdoors, natural history, and the precise observations of science. Hemingway filled notebooks with inventories of his property and other aspects of life ("1 worn out suit of clothes, 1 pair of hiking shoes . . . 1 Lot of knowledge about Woodcraft. Hunting. Fishing etc. 1 Lot of knowledge about farming, Lumbering"). But later, literature and writing, some of it very much informed by that scientific curiosity, took hold.

Over the summer, Hemingway got a piece of useful advice from Trumbull White, a family friend and retired magazine editor. White managed the Bay View Chautauqua near Petoskey, where Marcelline spent a month playing music. At a party, White told Hemingway that one learned to write by writing. And a newspaper job was just what the boy needed to learn about writing through experience.

In the end, newspapering made sense. He had taken to writing in high school. He crafted Ring Lardner knockoffs for the high school newspaper and, inexplicably inspired by a pawnbroker's sign, if not Lardner's penchant for wordplay, christened himself Hemingstein. He'd worked as a delivery boy for the local weekly paper, *Oak Leaves*. The family's house was filled with books and magazines, and Hemingway read them all. Marcelline said she and her brother both submitted essays to the *Atlantic Monthly* contributors club but were unsuccessful. Hemingway had a solid image of what writing professionally would mean to him. He had read Richard Harding Davis's book *Stories for Boys*, which contained an entertaining fantasy portrait of a newspaperman. In "The Reporter Who Made Himself King," Davis, a war correspondent who had died in 1916 while Hemingway was still in high school, spelled out the glamorous attraction of newspaper work. If Hemingway were looking for a way to grow up fast, he might have found a solution here:

> After three years—it is sometimes longer, sometimes not so long—he finds out that he has given his nerves and his youth and his enthusiasm in exchange for a general fund of miscellaneous knowledge, the opportunity of personal encounter with all the greatest and most remarkable men and events that have risen in those three years, and a great fund of resource and patience. He will find that he has crowded the experiences of the lifetime of the ordinary young business man, doctor, or lawyer, or man about town, into three short years; that he has learned to think and to act quickly, to be patient and unmoved when everyone else has lost his head, actually or figuratively speaking; to write as fast as another man can talk, and to be able to talk with authority on matters of which other men do not venture even to think until they have read what he has written.

The personal encounter with remarkable men, the fast writing—these were not empty words, as Hemingway would soon discover. But all that lay ahead. That summer he battled trout and dug potatoes at Longfield Farm; there was a brawl he took part in. Ernest didn't seem to be thinking much farther ahead than the moments of work and play that engaged him.

By August, Clarence Hemingway was disgusted. Grace was back in Oak Park, and he had his hands full with his son. "Ernest . . . is just as headstrong and abusive and threatening as ever," he wrote to his wife. We can suspect the teenager was testing his freedom and spending far more time with his friends than with his father.

Clarence had been urging Ernest to write to Uncle Leicester and to make up his mind about Kansas City. Tyler had been up for a visit just the week before, so clearly the subject was fresh. "Brother Tyler told him he could get Ernest a job on the Kansas City Star and Ernest could live at his house until he was well started."

For the next two months, Ernest worked the fields. He supplied Mrs. Dilworth's Pinehurst resort with potatoes but was worried over the poor quality of much of the crop. He vowed that he'd return to Oak Park the first week of October, in time for the World Series. And the woods, the fish, the lake became fixed in his mind. The red and yellow leaves of fall began to paint the background. Hemingway suffered a bout of tonsillitis and a headache after working in a carrot patch in the rain. He saw a doctor in Petoskey, who advised a little rest. His letters that September detail a heavy workload on the farm, but he recovered and soon reported to his father, "I am in great shape now and feeling lots of the old Jazz." He loaded a batch of apples and potatoes onto a lake boat to send to Oak Park, and his friendlier dispatches perhaps helped to smooth over the tensions. One day he landed a rainbow trout that measured seven pounds, nine ounces, big enough to put on display at Bump and McCabe's hardware store in Petoskey and win him a best-of-the-season prize. This summer—the beginning of his eighteenth year—added indelible details to the storehouse of material that he would eventually draw from and reimagine, off in another place when his life would have changed, when the wounds were real and when writing had become the fiber of his being.

Late in September, in response to Fannie Biggs's letters of recommendation, the managing editors of the *Chicago Examiner* and the *Chicago Daily Tribune* said they weren't hiring. One suggested sending Hemingway over anyway. By then, though, Hemingway saw his best life choice for now would be Kansas City. He left the lake on October 5, getting home in time to revel in Happy Felsch's fourth-inning home run for the victorious Chicago White Sox in the first game of the World Series against the New York Giants. Ten days later, on the morning of October 15, 1917, a Monday, Hemingway's father saw him off at the LaSalle Street Station in Chicago. We can turn to Hemingway's later fiction to find a pertinent reflection on that moment of departure:

> Robert Jordan had not felt this young since he had taken the train at Red Lodge to go down to Billings to get the train there to go away to school for the first time. He had been afraid to go and he did not want any one to know it and, at the station, just before the conductor picked up the box he would step up on to reach the steps of the day coach, his father had kissed him good-by and said, "May the Lord watch between thee and me while we are absent the one from the other." His father had been a very religious man and he had said it simply and sincerely. But his moustache had been moist and his eyes were damp with emotion and Robert Jordan had been so embarrassed by all of it, the damp religious sound of the prayer, and by his father kissing him good-by, that he had suddenly felt so much older than his father and sorry for him that he could hardly bear it.

It's possible to think that, like Robert Jordan going off to school, Hemingway might have been a little bit scared about leaving home and taking on his first job at a major American newspaper. Yet one must always read Hemingway's fiction as something other than biographical facts wrapped in invented names and situations. The best writing, he'd later say, was the stuff he made up. But as Hemingway wrote that passage in *For Whom the Bell Tolls*, he might very well have looked back at that transformative moment and thought of himself as "so much older than his father," a man who, a decade later, would deeply disappoint his son by taking his own life.

Similarly, if we can believe that a short, unfinished sketch about a young man on a train has some grounding in fact, then Ernest Hemingway thought about baseball as the train to Kansas City sat at a siding on the east side of the Mississippi River. On this day, while traveling toward his new life away from home, the White Sox played in New York. In the sketch "Crossing the Mississippi," Nick Adams, Hemingway's frequent alter ego, learns from a roving magazine vendor on the train—"Got any dope on the Series?" he'd asked—that the White Sox had won the last game. That puts a "comfortable glow," a "fine feeling" on the last leg of the trip, and he sits back to read his *Saturday Evening Post* as the train rumbles westward across Missouri.

Crossing the river might very well have been a strong metaphor for Hemingway, a meaningful passage from one stage of life to another, from rambunctiousness, perhaps, to a kind of maturity he'd find as a newsman. And crossing the Mississippi on his way to Kansas City triggered Hemingway's thoughts of history and a writer he long admired. "Mark Twain, Huck Finn, Tom Sawyer, and LaSalle crowded each other in Nick's mind as he looked up the flat, brown plain of slow-moving water. Anyhow I've seen the Mississippi, he thought happily to himself."

Hemingway's stories about Nick Adams parallel his own biography geographically, socially, psychologically. There are stories set in Petoskey, Horton Bay, and the Michigan woods and streams; there are stories about Nick and his parents and stories about Nick and his wounding in the Italian war. None of the Nick Adams stories, however, place him in Kansas City. That brief period in 1917–18 is a void in the cycle of Nick's fictional chronicles, the void between growing up and going to war. One can speculate why Hemingway never filled that gap, though Hemingway's sister

Marcelline believed that the Nick Adams stories reflected the experiences of a fellow reporter he listened to in Kansas City. Whether her observation was based on knowledge, on something Hemingway told her, on conjecture, or on a desire to protect her family's reputation remains unclear. But it suggests the idea that Kansas City had in fact lodged itself in Hemingway's consciousness.

Kansas City certainly would give Hemingway the confidence to find his identity as a writer. As he landed in town he had to embrace the words of his friend Lucille Dick. "Oh Oinest," she'd written early in October, "don't let money lure you with its golden gleams into being a working man—you know you are much better fitted to be a newspaper man than anything else. Your writing is so clever—so easy and so really fine that it would be a crime for you not to make the most of your talents. Don't bury them—put them out at interest."

When Ernest stepped off the Chicago train and onto the platform at Kansas City's Union Station on October 15, 1917, he left behind his summer of indecision. As he waited to meet up with his uncle Tyler, he must have been teeming with conflicting emotions. His senses surely felt the brashness of freedom and the awesome sense of something new and untried and leading to who knows what. His family was five hundred miles behind him, though his uncle represented a prickly branch that he would deal with as swiftly as possible. And then he would truly be on his own, making his own way, becoming a man, mining his self-described lode of "natural ability," crafting a future that perhaps even he could not foresee.

2

CREATIVE CAULDRON

Every man on the paper from top to bottom was convinced
of his own right to express himself unhampered,
save by the truth as he saw it.
—WILLIAM ALLEN WHITE

The clack of typing mills and the smoke of countless cigars filled the vast open newsroom of the *Kansas City Star* day and night. With a morning paper, an afternoon edition, and a regional weekly delivered to a farm audience across the country, the *Star*'s staff members toiled in the room from before 8:00 AM to well after midnight. Ernest Hemingway, a young newcomer to the business, walked into this second-floor beehive in mid-October 1917 to begin his apprenticeship in journalism. He had some high school newspaper writing under his belt, but this was the big time—the *Star* was one of the best-known and most well-regarded newspapers in the country. For his first month, he'd take home a probationary fifteen dollars a week, a little low on the scale of professional expectations but an accomplishment for the young man from Oak Park, Illinois.

Hemingway's entrée into the business came through his uncle, Alfred Tyler Hemingway. Tyler Hemingway, an executive in the lumber industry, had been a classmate at Oberlin of Henry J. Haskell, the *Star*'s chief editorial writer. After Hemingway arrived from Chicago, as cooler weather was settling in on that Monday afternoon, his uncle undoubtedly gave the young man his opinions about Haskell and the newspaper. Hemingway thought his uncle was pompous and annoying, so he hardly listened and figured he'd do what he always did, which was satisfy his own urges to learn and explore and embrace the pleasures of life in the bustling city and the buzzing newsroom.

Hemingway's buddy Carl Edgar, the friend he'd newly made in Michigan, had met him at the vast Union Station, and they surely had a grand reunion as they talked about what the near future would bring. When he eventually got to his uncle's Victorian home on Warwick Boulevard, Hemingway would have eagerly settled in with the five o'clock edition of the *Star*, which carried the sweet news from the World Series in New York. Sox Win the Title, the bold headline read, right there on the front page. The line score, 4–2, and even the box score from the game, which an avid Sox fan would have savored word for word, number by number, appeared at the top of the page. The box made it clear that a three-run fourth inning and a dominant performance by pitcher Red Faber were all the Chicago team needed to conquer the Giants. The front page had it all. A game summary and an inning-by-inning account of the action completed the coverage.

Hemingway arrived in Kansas City two years after the death of the *Star*'s influential founder, William Rockhill Nelson, and soon enough he'd hear about "the Colonel" from the newspaper veterans who had worked for him. Nelson had come to Kansas City from Fort Wayne, Indiana, and, with a partner, launched the *Kansas City Evening Star* in 1880. He built it into a strong and persuasive civic voice concerned with improving the city and informing and educating its citizens, though not in a preachy way.

Nelson sought to communicate with "all kinds of readers," but the most valuable readers, he once wrote to his staff, were "the thirty thousand who do the thinking." Among other progressive notions, Nelson championed what came to be known as the City Beautiful Movement, and his campaign on behalf of an extensive parks and boulevard system in the 1890s helped shape the layout and landscape of the city in perpetuity. He was "the most dominant factor in awakening the young city's civic consciousness." Nelson had amassed great wealth and showed it in a palatial home he built on twenty acres about two miles south of the newspaper office. He was broad beamed and had an imperious-looking face that managed to appear spherical and squared-up at the same time. He could speak gently to staffers or get wound up with passion. "Nelson was a stormy, dominating figure," William Allen White, a *Star* man who went on to become the famous editor of the *Emporia (Kansas) Gazette*, wrote years later. "He became the most adored and the best hated leader of the Middle West. There was no neutral feeling toward him."

As a news organization, Nelson's *Star* hewed to civility, erudition, and thoroughness. "Nelson despised shabbiness and disorder," and that ethos carried over to the news coverage in his paper. "Always keep in mind the family that pays 10 cents a week for our paper," he advised his editors. He urged them to make the paper so complete for its readers that if "your family were marooned on Robinson Crusoe's island for a year without books, or magazines, and still could be served twice a day by carrier pigeons with the *Star*, you would feel that you hadn't missed a thing in the way of news, current or standard literature, fashions, gossip, comment, or what not." His staff members, who wrote without bylines generally until the 1930s, were proud to have their work appear as the collective voice of the *Star*. "Virtually everyone on the staff was so thoroughly imbued with Nelson's ideals that they accepted his programs without question—even fought for them. *The Star* was their bible. They swore by it; and many believed there was no other newspaper worthy of their talents." In a roomful of skeptics and strivers, there were, of course, exceptions. And some of the more ambitious talents discovered a truth about the limits of Nelson's loyalty. Sumner Blossom, a small and wiry cigar chewer and future magazine editor, spent four years at the *Star* in the 1910s, until he told Nelson he'd been offered a job elsewhere. He didn't want to leave, but he thought he deserved more money. Nelson agreed, but with a sting: "You are worth more to them, but not to me," he said, adding that he would give Blossom a letter of recommendation to the *New York World*, the *Chicago Tribune*, or anywhere else. "The *Star* has an endless supply of young talent that others haven't got."

Hemingway, in his six and a half months at the newspaper, was a piece of that endless supply of talent. He certainly heard some of the rah-rah stories of the *Star*. Nelson was gone by then, but his spirit remained in the paper's outlook and self-image. Nelson had "no patience with conventionality," and he liked work that was "original, imaginative, entertaining, but above all clearly written." He preferred liveliness, though not faddish language, over solemn and stodgy writing. As one staffer put it, "If a reporter was doing a really different and intelligible job the policy of the paper used to be to forget the rules and give him his head." The *Star* was a place for independent thinkers and focused talents who could thrive in that atmosphere, a place built on a foundation of education and culture. In the general absence of journalism schools, "the *Star* itself was a training school and some of its editors were excellent teachers. Their methods usually left the new reporter to find the way by himself—turned loose at the outset to see what he could do." Young newcomers to the newsroom did not go through a painstaking indoctrination into news writing. "Originality counted here above all else," a veteran reporter once recalled. A new reporter was allowed to find his own voice. However, while doing so he usually had to successfully conquer obituary writing and maybe a bit of church news before breaking into the ranks of the general assignment reporter.

Alongside the news of the World Series, the *Star* on that day of Hemingway's arrival offered a valuable introduction to the world he was about to enter. In the column next to the game coverage, an item announced that a well-known local minister, just back from Europe, would be writing of the action in Italy, "where he had exceptional opportunities to view the war from that angle." The Rev. Dr. Burris A. Jenkins had gotten home to Kansas City the day before, and along with this promotional note that he would deliver a series of articles, another front-page story reported on his observation of conditions near the front, where "evil influences" from nearby cities caused concern for military camps. "When a British soldier contracts a loathsome disease," said Jenkins, also a representative of the YMCA, "he is ordered immediately into the front line trenches with the expectation that he will be killed in the next attack." Inside the paper, in another long dispatch he had filed from France, Jenkins compared a French battlefield victory to the glorious memory of Gettysburg. Given a byline, Jenkins clearly was someone with clout in Kansas City. In the coming weeks, Hemingway would learn much from him about writing and war.

The news of the day also reported that the Germans were advancing in the Gulf of Riga, pressuring the Russians. An illustration displayed the capability of a German shell: the twisted wreckage of a motorcar sat atop a house near Verdun. There was an item about the impending and locally controversial movement of twelve thousand "Negro draftees" to Camp Funston, an army installation a few hours west of Kansas City, where a valley had been transformed into a believably accurate network of trenches, complete with barbed wire, bombproof shelters, dressing stations, and tunnels.

As for local news, Hemingway might have gotten a sense of Kansas City's rough-and-tumble atmosphere in a story about a string of home and business burglaries. By contrast, all the downtown hotel rooms had been booked for the last week of the month in advance of a convention of churchgoers. One could almost hear Hemingway, as he tried to do in one letter home, reassuring his mother that, despite her concerns about her son's independence, the Christian influence was indeed present in his new surroundings.

On Wednesday, October 17, Hemingway entered the formidable newsman's haven at a time of transition, as the newspaper's quaint ways were being displaced by the "alarums of war." *Star* men were leaving for the war at a brisk rate, faster than they could be replaced with experienced reporters. The city editor, George Longan, resorted to finding men whose single qualification was that they could type. Hemingway wasn't the smoothest at it, but he would do for the moment. Surely he'd have no trouble with the routine work he'd be expected to do. As a cub reporter, he'd start with some grunt tasks: compiling letters to the editor and checking with funeral homes for deaths of notable locals, whose obituaries might amount to a concise paragraph in the paper. The "undertakers route" meant calling or visiting ten or so of the better-known mortuaries, several of them within walking distance of the *Star*. Russel Crouse, a future playwright working at the *Star* at the time, once teased a young reporter about the need to put "more life" into his obits. So the young man came back with this one: "It had always been the wish of Mr. and Mrs. Henry Jones that they die together. Half the wish was fulfilled yesterday when Mr. Jones died." Crouse had been a sports writer, on the road with the Blues baseball team that year, but was called back to the office to help shore up the newsroom as staffers went to war.

Despite the sense of freedom that Nelson's *Star* fostered, the newsroom, by the time Hemingway arrived, did not operate without certain fundamentals and rules. The method was drummed into his head: spell the names correctly, get all the facts straight, aspire to tell a story. *Star* editors had compiled a long list of style reminders. For years it was a word-of-mouth production, but by 1915 it became a printed sheet that laid out 110 rules to write by. Its first few lines would become famous in Hemingway and journalism lore: "Use short sentences. Use short first paragraphs. Use vigorous English. Be positive, not negative." Of course many of its guidelines remain commonsense approaches to good writing: "Never use old slang. . . . Watch your sequence of tenses. . . . Eliminate every superfluous word." To some, the rules were irritants but certainly not obstacles. "All *Star* desk men were full of don'ts," said one reporter. "It took longer to find out what you could not put into the paper than what you could put in."

If Hemingway was self-conscious about being a ruddy-cheeked newcomer straight out of high school, it helped to learn that Longan, the city editor, had never gone to college either. Longan, too, had been only eighteen when he started as a reporter, at four dollars a week, for the *Kansas City Times* in 1897, a few years before Nelson acquired that paper and, though he preserved its name, turned it into the *Star*'s morning edition. Hemingway handed Longan his uncle's letter of introduction, and Longan had heard a word about the new young man from Henry Haskell. Longan, large of body and squeaky of voice, was a sharp newsman, personable, enthusiastic, willing to give a story "both barrels" if it seemed promising, "and had to be cooled off occasionally by some of the more conservative executives." Of course, all staffers learned of Longan's idiosyncratic phobia: no story would ever be allowed to mention the word *snake*. Legend had it that he once fired a man who had the misfortune of rolling up his sleeves one afternoon, revealing tattooed serpents on each arm.

Longan and his assistant, C. G. "Pete" Wellington, would have pointed Hemingway toward an empty seat to wait for his first assignment, and the young man soon was made to feel at home as he met some of his new colleagues. "His arms and legs were too long for his suit," Dale Wilson recalled. "But his tanned face was pleasant, his eyes twinkled. The new boy got a casual welcome. Leo Fitzpatrick, Peg Vaughn, Wilson Hicks, Todd Ormiston, Punk Wallace, Bill Moorhead, Harry Godfrey, John Collings, Harry Kohr and the rest of us who were nearby shook his hand. But the greeting given by H. Merle Smith, fresh out of the University of Kansas, outdid all others. His eyes concentrating on the stranger, Smith pumped his hand in the fraternity-rushing, super-salesman manner. That was the beginning of Hemingway's favorite name for him—'Smith the Beamer.'"

A typical rookie assignment that day would have appealed to the baseball fan from Chicago. An editor called for fashioning a small item of self-serving importance to the newspaper. Like almost everything else, it carried no byline, so there's no way to confirm its authorship. But Wellington handed a reporter a brief piece of correspondence and asked for this news lead to introduce it:

In the world's baseball series, The Star furnished the Eighty-ninth Division at Camp Funston with a telegraphic report on all of the games, received direct from the scene of operations. The following letter was received today from Maj. Gen. Leonard Wood, commanding the Eighty-ninth.

The Editor, Kansas City Star: The furnishing of the baseball returns by your paper, by means of a scoreboard, was a source of a great deal of pleasure to a large number of men of the National

Army. It gives me pleasure to express to you my appreciation of this service. Assuring you that your service was very much appreciated by both officers and men of this command, I remain yours very truly, Leonard Wood, Major General, U.S.A.

This was not the most prominent piece of news in the paper, but it had its place amid the densely packed sea of type that amounted to the *Star's* daily report. And Hemingway certainly would become aware of General Wood, dropping his name in at least one letter home. As the day progressed, Hemingway's colleagues gathered news from the wires and from their beats. Nestling against ads for Union suits, baking powder, department store specials, and Robert Burns Cigars, the war as a subject was pervasive throughout the paper. A front-page story reported on the lagging drives for a "war camp fund" and Liberty Bonds. The editorial page carried a literary feature from the *New York Tribune* on America's naval destroyers, which stealthily went about the task of war; LEAN GREYHOUNDS OF THE SEA MERCILESSLY TRAIL U-BOATS, read the headline. "So far the god of battles being kind, none of our destroyers has received the terrible christening of the life blood of one of her crew, but each day the ships shave danger and eventually it will come." Nearby, the op-ed page reflected the *Star's* practice of presenting works of contemporary literature, and this October brought a serialization of *The Kingdom of the Blind*, a war novel by E. Phillips Oppenheim, originally published in 1916. Elsewhere a pictorial layout, based on photographs, showed American troops training in France: "A Chasseur inspecting rifles"; "Learning to dig a trench"; "Learning to throw bombs"; "A camouflaged tent." "Bombing and trench digging," the caption read, "are two of the most important things to know in the style of fighting to which the American troops will devote themselves."

Hemingway that first afternoon encountered another long article by Burris Jenkins, this one reporting on Champagne and environs: "Of all the sad sights along the French frontier," he wrote, "there is nothing sadder than the once beautiful city of Reims." Another element of the Jenkins layout caught Hemingway's eye that day. It was a reproduction of Jenkins's press credentials, hard to miss given that it spanned three columns. The image of the document, with his portrait and signature, affirmed Jenkins's status as a foreign correspondent and reinforced the idea of authority and experience that Richard Harding Davis had implanted in Hemingway's imagination.

Other recent pieces by Jenkins brought readers intimate detail of daily life along the western front, laying the foundation for the arrival of American troops and what their communities and families might expect. The previous Sunday's paper included another panel of sketches about PERSHING'S MEN IN FRANCE and a Jenkins column with an unusual headline: CUPID OUTRANKS MARS IN PERSHING'S ARMY. In that one, Jenkins suggested that if they didn't die in battle—giving "rich, young American blood" for the land of Lafayette—the newly arrived soldiers from the United States might stick around in France for the women. But there was a somber and patriotic side to Jenkins's account, too: "They will go grimly through the task given them to perform, the task of rendering war impossible and unnecessary for their sons and their sons' sons, that they, in turn may give their fighting qualities to the causes of freedom and democracy, the solution of the problems of peace, the betterment of humanity, the ideals toward which the world is blindly groping upward through mud and blood and smoke." This was the sort of idealism and faith in the cause of war that Hemingway eventually would write against on the other side of his own war experience. But Jenkins's reports about the European fronts that appeared in the *Star* gave readers like Hemingway solid evidence of how details from war zones can be gathered and framed within a seasoned and authoritative point of view.

Along with the editors who aimed to control Hemingway's daily workflow and to grow him into a real writer, Jenkins was one of two important outside figures who loom over the young man's introduction to professional journalism and writing about war in Kansas City. The other was Theodore Roosevelt, the former president and Hemingway's boyhood hero. Through his earlier political connections and friendship with Nelson, Roosevelt had been commissioned to write editorials for the *Star*, and the pieces were subsequently picked up by more than fifty papers around the country. In the Sunday paper that week, Roosevelt argued that the War Department had been too slow to order rifles the previous spring, and as of October 2 there were only one hundred rifles for every twenty thousand men. "Surely," he wrote, "if there is anything this war teaches it is the vital importance of time." Roosevelt's ongoing arguments with President Woodrow Wilson appeared throughout Hemingway's Kansas City apprenticeship. Hemingway's boyhood expectation of joining the war effort evolved during his months in Kansas City, and Roosevelt's editorials offered the ring of patriotism balanced by outspoken criticism that would have appealed to Hemingway's cynical side.

It was still relatively warm, in the seventies, with rain in the air and a cold front on the way, when Hemingway left the office after his first day on the job. The streetcar back to his uncle's place passed the business life of Main Street along the way. He would have seen Carl Edgar's office, the California Fuel Oil Co., on Main just south of Thirty-First Street. With echoes of the newsroom in Hemingway's head—the handshakes with new friends, the voice of Wellington (*Mr. Hemingway, would you . . . ?*)—his lanky frame carried a bounce that evening. He had to be feeling good about himself and his future. After dinner with his uncle, his aunt, and

This snapshot of Theodore Roosevelt and William Rockhill Nelson appeared as the frontispiece in an anthology of Roosevelt's columns for the *Kansas City Star*. *Photographer unknown*

two cousins, the young newspaper reporter dutifully sat down with a piece of paper and wrote a brief note to his parents. His trip was fine; he was happy to have Carl Edgar around, and they planned eventually to room together; he'd work from eight till five, six days a week; the relatives send their love. "Today I had 3 stories in the star," he wrote. "It seems like a pretty good paper. They have a very big plant."

Not much in the way of details. Hemingway rarely told his parents everything. And his missive delivered a rather understated account of his entry into the roar and discipline of reporting and writing. In his first critical biography of Hemingway, Carlos Baker, echoing Herman Melville's appraisal that the sea had been "his Harvard and his Yale," asserted that Hemingway's "college and gradus ad Parnassum was the continent of Europe." Perhaps he meant that Europe was Hemingway's graduate school. On this day in October 1917, the newsroom equivalent of Hemingway's college education was now fully under way.

3

"THE MORALLY STRENUOUS LIFE"

It is the height of silliness to go into newspaper stuff I have written,
which has nothing to do with the other writing.
—Ernest Hemingway to bibliographer Louis Henry Cohn

The young Hemingway suffered in his uncle's presence. He had little use for the man, who he thought was "a vain, pompous man absorbed in his own grandeur and wholly lacking in a sense of humor." Uncle Tyler, an uninspiring businessman, reminded Hemingway of many of the things he disliked in his own father, Tyler's brother. His father had taught him so much about science and nature, but he was insufferably inadequate as a role model, pedantic, conventional, moralistic. And now how long would Ernest have to be grateful to his uncle, the man who got him his start as a newspaper reporter?

If Hemingway needed kindling to fuel his quiet animosity toward his uncle, he had only to look through the pages of Tyler's own writings. He'd recently published a little book of business optimism, titled *How to Make Good*. There was plenty to amp up the young man's sarcastic demeanor and to affirm his own decision to test his career mettle in journalism. The chapter headings were filled with commonsense platitudes: "Determine to Succeed," "Be Straightforward," "Apply the Spurs to Yourself." The book was a testament not just to making money but also to attaining happiness all around you. "No life is complete that does not contribute to the happiness of others," he wrote. To read his uncle's litany of decorum and level thinking is to encounter the very opposite of how Hemingway carried on in life. Hemingway apparently could not muster the sort of generous spirit with which the *Star* itself regarded his uncle. When Tyler Hemingway died just four years later, a *Star* editorialist, probably Henry Haskell, praised him as a good-humored man who "loved life," a man known for his business savvy and his civic contributions: "He was not too busy to serve his church, to serve the cause of education, to take part in municipal progress."

At a time when Hemingway's figurative wings were spreading, the setting was oppressive. So Hemingway had no intention of spending much more time at his aunt and uncle's home. Within a few days, he took a room in a boardinghouse a block to the south on Warwick Boulevard. Miss Gertrude Haynes's big stone mansion at 3733 Warwick gave Ernest cover and a taste of real adult freedom. Still, he figured sometime soon he'd be sharing rooms elsewhere with Carl Edgar. For one thing Miss Haynes's rate was more than half his first month's probationary salary of sixty dollars. "Everybody at the Star says 35 a month for two meals and a bed is Robbry," he told his father.

Kansas City, as Hemingway found it, was a prosperous city at the junction of two rivers. It was notably smaller than Chicago but shared some of the same characteristics. Among its three hundred thousand citizens there were haves and have-nots. There were political shenanigans and hints of corruption. There was the odorous bustle of stockyards, which sprawled over the riverside flats west of downtown, and the gritty exhalations of freight and passenger trains. Lumber was big among the swells, including Uncle Tyler, who worked for his father-in-law, John Barber White, at a prominent company that owned vast forest lands and reaped the harvest. The city was shaped, too, by the grain and cattle trades and by the railroads. Its burgeoning refinement came largely from the upper classes and from those who controlled the rolling land-scape and developed the growing city's real estate possibilities, as the *Star*'s late publisher, William Rockhill Nelson, had done in the acreage around his huge mansion at Forty-Fifth Street. One real estate man, J. C. Nichols, was in the process of platting a huge swath in the southwest stretch of the city, even into neighboring Kansas. Nichols envisioned parks and shopping districts mod-eled on English villages and fine homes of restricted ownership, available, that is, for occupancy by the white upper crust of the Christian persuasion.

The daily papers, with their abundance of short items and boldfaced headlines on the front page, kept track of who was giving to the war bond effort and how much was yet needed to be raised. The city's nightly entertainment offered William S. Hart at the movies or the likes of a visiting prodigy, the violinist Jascha Heifetz, in a concert hall. In the rougher precincts one could find numerous other kinds of entertainment. Dance halls blazing with the racy and new jazz music advertised in the *Star*'s columns. And the police news recorded raids on "immoral resorts," North-End knifings, and other criminal activities. Morris Kallish, the proprietor of the Rex Hotel on Eighth Street, made the news one day when he was fined $200 for inducing twenty-year-old Sophie West from New York with a promise of police protection "in an immoral life." (The court ordered West and three other women to pay $100 each, and she was paroled to the welfare board.) In due course Hemingway would be exposed to this netherworld by way of the newsroom's daily assignment sheet and his own extracurricular interest in hanging out with ambulance surgeons and other streetwise authorities.

Kansas City was a brawny place, whose edges and rolling terrain were defined by limestone outcroppings and towering bluffs. Early pioneers had cut through the northernmost bluffs above the Missouri River to lay roads and build hillside houses. The city grew southward from the river to meet up with and finally consume the settlement of Westport, where outfitters had sent travelers on the Santa Fe, California, Mormon, and Oregon Trails. Hemingway's Kansas City stretched forty blocks or more from the North End, where city hall and police headquarters stood in his day, past the *Star's* impressive brick headquarters on Grand, and on to the Hyde Park neighborhood, where his uncle and other relatives lived, and even farther south. The city's place on the border of the western frontier and at the meeting of North and South helped define Kansas City's "remarkably intense and sometimes violent character."

Within a few days, Hemingway sent his father a couple of items, roughly torn from the paper, evidence that he indeed was gainfully employed in the business of recording the life of his new city. As with everything he would write in the next six and a half months, none of these bits carried his byline. The practice of anonymity enforced the idea that the paper projected the voice of the *Star* in its columns, except in those special occasions saved for celebrity writers such as Burris Jenkins and Theodore Roosevelt. Two of Hemingway's items (complete with typos) comprised a single paragraph; the third stretched to four. One story announced the opening of a conference of "Negro Methodist Episcopal" churchgoers. Another reported on the hospitalization of an assistant fire chief, "who was run down by a motor car."

The *Star* was surrounded by car dealerships, tire sellers, and automotive shops, all reflecting the rise of motorcar culture and, in Chief John J. Vaughn's case, its accompanying dangers. Hemingway also reported on a city council effort to wrestle with the new vehicular technology: "Glaring motor car headlights will not be banned from Kansas City if the new ordinance introduced by motor dealers in the city council a week ago becomes a law."

Surely Hemingway felt a certain pride in recognizing that his first journalistic efforts appeared on the same pages as Theodore Roosevelt's pointed commentaries. Roosevelt, the former Rough Rider, adventurer, and political flamethrower, was Hemingway's boyhood inspiration. Curiously, Hemingway never mentioned Roosevelt in his letters to family that fall. But perhaps he identified with the letter writer in the *Star* one day who stood up for Roosevelt in the face of criticism. The writer, a Boy Scout patrol leader, liked that Roosevelt was "a fighting man": "We are taught to keep away from cowards and liars and to admire the man who dares speak the truth and back it up with his life—the man who is ready to sacrifice his life and give the country the services of his sons." Roosevelt had set the stage for Hemingway's passage to adulthood, a point that Michael Reynolds makes repeatedly in the first volume of his five-book biography. "Belief and enthusiasm, Roosevelt said, were the keys: without them there was little chance of doing 'a man's work in the world.'" Hemingway's values, as they would emerge later in his fiction, were "courage, love, honor, self-reliance, work and duty. They were the same values that Teddy Roosevelt lived by and advocated; they are the basis for the morally strenuous life."

After the United States entered the war in April 1917 and its dangers for American lives became real, Roosevelt had promoted the creation of a volunteer force to aid the fight in France and had also urged citizens to serve in whatever way they could: "Let him, if a man of fighting age, do his utmost to get into the fighting line—Red Cross work, Y.M.C.A. work, driving ambulances, and the like, excellent though it all is, should be left to men not of military age or unfit for military service, and to women; young men of vigorous bodies and sound hearts should be left free to do their proper work in the fighting line." Roosevelt's call certainly would resonate with Hemingway as his desire for war experience evolved in the coming months. Though his father had adamantly opposed military service for him, Hemingway would have found a more rational voice coming from Roosevelt.

On Tuesday, October 23, two of Roosevelt's columns appeared in the papers, one in the morning and one in the afternoon. In the morning, on the front page, Roosevelt expressed his "regret with bitter shame the folly of our government in dawdling and delaying for six vital months after the German note of January 31 last before seriously beginning the work of building big, swift cargo boats." Roosevelt had hoped that "hundreds of thousands of men" would already be "in the firing line" on the way to having two million or more soldiers in Europe by the following year. Roosevelt wanted nothing less than the utter defeat of Germany, and he belittled pacifists and others agitating for a "premature peace." His war cry was forceful and alarming: "We must now fight with all our might on European soil beside our allies or else fear the day when we will have to fight without allies beside our burning homes." Hemingway had begun dropping hints to his sister in letters about his intention to join the war effort, angling to be among those two million in Europe. Roosevelt in the *Star*, if only unconsciously, contributed to his position. Roosevelt's version of the "morally strenuous life" still represented to young Hemingway a sharp contrast to Uncle Tyler's finger-wagging prescriptions to avoid "secret rottenness." Within days of Roosevelt's October 23 columns, Hemingway joined the Seventh Regiment of the Missouri Guard.

The next Roosevelt column appeared in the first afternoon edition of the paper that day. This one included the observation that the horrendous toll of men injured in the war could be addressed with better efforts of reconstructive surgery in order to "make the cripple less of a burden to himself and others." Military and health leaders had plans for the "curative workshop." As the son of a doctor and with a strong interest in science and medicine, Hemingway understood the progressive and restorative nature of these plans. "The purpose," Roosevelt wrote, "is to insist that every man, no matter how maimed shall be made of further use in the world." Just nine months in the future, Hemingway would face that reality of war.

That evening, as Hemingway headed home from the newsroom, a throng watched a "liberty beacon" blaze on the hillside south of Union Station, a celebration to highlight Liberty Bond Day throughout the region and a prelude to a huge parade planned the next day in Kansas City. Patriotic speeches and a blaring band whipped up the crowd. A mound of boxes and barrels, carted to the site by the wagonload, stood ready to go up in flames at 7:30 PM, awaiting the match applied by the city's acting mayor, Albert I. Beach. The next day, more throngs gathered to view the parade and filled the streets with joyful noise for hours afterward. They clogged the Twelfth Street spine on a weekday afternoon even more densely than on a rowdy Saturday night. "They knew they had accomplished something," a *Star* reporter wrote. "Bonds, patriotism, money, men and nameless other things, and loud cheers proclaimed it."

Hemingway had fancied himself a boxer in high school, and his interest in the sport accompanied him to Kansas City. On the sports page one day, he noticed news of Bob Fitzsimmons's death. The *Star's* unsigned Umpire column recounted the late boxer's life and ended with an assessment of how legends gather power, an observation that might have meant something to a writer seeking a reputation: "Speckled Robert could hit harder than any man of his day. A few years after his passing as a champion history had him hitting like a sledge hammer. A few years later the sledge hammer wallop had assumed the proportion of a battering ram blow. A few more years now and fight bugs will be referring to the Fitzsimmons punch as fistiana's French seventy-fiver." *Fistiana*. That kind of wordplay agreed with Hemingway, the great Hemingstein, the old Brute ("brother"), the joshing correspondent who was always communicating with his siblings and friends in verbal code and comic language. He didn't merely write letters to an elected close friend; he "indicts this epistle." Though the *Star's* editors frowned upon slang, a sense of creative vernacular sprang through when appropriate. And sports writers, Hemingway's hero Ring Lardner among them, always find a way to have fun.

The next item in the Umpire column continued a fascination with Fitzsimmons. It carried the touch of a writer who might have been familiar with Joseph Conrad's *Heart of Darkness*, published the year Hemingway was born. The newsroom was filled with literary men, cultured readers who had designs on writing their own novels, and perhaps one of them produced this, with its echo of Conrad's line "Mistah Kurtz—he dead":

The death of Bob Fitzsimmons recalled to a Kansas City man a laconic message that a Kansas City fistic follower who attended the fight at Carson City sent to a friend who couldn't make the trip. The wire was a model of brevity as follows:

"Fitz—he win."

Those three words afford a study in sentiment.

Are they indicative of elation? Was the sender of the message a Fitzsimmons man?

Or does the brief wire register disappointment—disgust? Fitz—he win.

Our guess is that the author of that telegram had a bet on James J. Corbett.

Hemingway later pronounced himself not much of an admirer of Conrad. But as he was learning now, the *Star*'s reporters, like the crafter of the Fitzsimmons item, could fashion a literary narrative in the briefest of tales. One police item early in his apprenticeship presented a model narrative, a lesson in the *Star* reporters' ethos that simple, declarative sentences should add up to a story worth telling. It's quite possible that this particular story was one of "six yarns in the sheet" that Hemingway boasted about writing that day:

Mrs. Ralph Wildbauhm, 1307 Broadway, planned to buy a Liberty Loan Bond today. She went to get $142 she had placed in a hole in the wall of her home. It was gone. She telephoned police headquarters. Arther Leppert, a patrolman, was sent to investigate. It was quiet, almost everyone in the neighborhood having gone to watch the parade. Leppert heard a scratching noise in an adjoining room. He entered and found a rat hole in the door. He removed some flooring and found a rat's abode, lined with currency.

Some of the bills were torn, but they were all there.

Mrs. Wildbauhm will get her Liberty Bond.

Furthering this literary training ground, excerpts of recent novels appeared daily on the op-ed pages, and book-related reflections popped up everywhere. An anonymous humor writer on the editorial page planted a literary seed for Hemingway in this "Starbeams" quip: "Fiction is where you read about the woman who returns his letters unopened." A feature story, reprinted from the *New York Evening Sun*, gave Hemingway a glimpse into the life of Lucie Lacoste, "a Cuban girl, who learned English and became a successful novelist in six years." She had a one-act play on the road, a book of verse, and a novel, *Miminetta*, on the market—"all published, in regular bindings and gilt letters and everything!" The accompanying portrait showed a determined and attractive "young Cuban rebel" who represented for the story's overeager writer an unusual example of a woman with fight and a mother who has it all: "Many an American writer would like to know the recipe for success that this young Cuban seems to have found for herself."

In those earliest days at the *Star*, if Hemingway were looking for evidence of what contributes to a journalist's success, he got a sample under the simple headline A GREAT REPORTER. This was an editorial page excerpt in a Kansas Notes column from the *Atchison Globe*. It praised Henry Allen, editor of the *Wichita Beacon*, whose letters from France had been appearing in the *Star*. The letters are "literature," the item said. "Besides that they are the real thing. No exaggerated statements, but the truth simply told by a man who knows how to write." (The next day the *Star* published a one-column picture of Henry Allen in a colonel's uniform, Casual Officers, USA, sent recently from Rome.)

The truth simply told by a man who knows how to write. That concise judgment presented a useful thought that Hemingway could file away and call on whenever he needed a reminder.

———————

Hemingway was lonely, he told his sister. He filled his time with work, and he and Carl Edgar found opportunities to "jazz forth with frequency." On Hemingway's first Sunday in Kansas City, he and Edgar hopped an electric car of the Interurban Railway for an outing to St. Joseph, about sixty miles to the north, to visit with his friend's family. If you can believe him, he dropped into the office of the *St. Joseph Gazette* and considered a job possibility though rejected it for the "mere pittance" of its pay. Still, to his sister, the subtext was loneliness in the quiet moments between work and jazzing forth.

One week after Hemingway began his new life, a stream of news from Europe began breaking, a turn in the war that would worm its way into his consciousness. As the front-page headline had it: STRIKING AT ITALY. Hemingway wouldn't have known it quite then, but this and subsequent dispatches would foretell of a defining chapter in his life and career.

4

"THE INSIGNIFICANCE
OF SELF"

I will go not because of any love of gold braid glory etc. but because
I couldn't face any body after the war and not have been in it.
—ERNEST HEMINGWAY, TO HIS SISTER MARCELLINE

B urris Atkins Jenkins was everywhere. After six months of
touring the war zones in Europe, Jenkins had returned home
to Kansas City on October 14, 1917, the day before Hemingway
arrived. The *Star* carried news of Jenkins's return. It touted a series
of his public lectures. It devoted considerable space to his reports
of the war zones in France and Italy. Jenkins was the well-spoken,
liberal pastor of one of Kansas City's most influential churches, the
Linwood Boulevard Christian Church. His mission to Europe had
been on behalf of the Young Men's Christian Association. He gave
pep talks to troops and surveyed problems of hygiene and morale
in the effort. He would go on to serve for a short time as editor
of a rival Kansas City newspaper, the *Post*, and to accumulate a
national audience with a radio program. In the mid-1920s, Sinclair
Lewis gave a provocative talk in Jenkins's church, and Kansas City

wound up providing a backdrop for *Elmer Gantry*, Lewis's novel of religious hucksterism (in contrast to a good and inspirational man like Jenkins). For Lewis, Hemingway, or any man of action of the era, it would not have been difficult to admire a spiritual leader whose lasting motto was "Live dangerously!"

On a Thursday that October, Jenkins sat among the VIPs at a luncheon of newspaper editors from the region. They had gathered in the plush dining hall of the Muehlebach Hotel to hear from Lord Northcliffe, the powerful British publisher. Jenkins listened closely as Northcliffe talked about the "long, hard war" ahead and what America's role ought to be. Enlisting soldiers was important, Northcliffe said, but moving them across the ocean was key to successful warfare.

Northcliffe had spent a good part of the morning with Irwin Kirkwood, publisher of the *Star* (and William Rockhill Nelson's son-in-law). Northcliffe sat on a sofa at Kirkwood's stately home for a detailed interview by a *Star* reporter destined for a write-up on page one that afternoon. He traced his points on the palm of his hand as he spoke and habitually removed and pocketed his eyeglasses, then put them back on. "Those who talk of a short war, whether in England or America, have not grasped the magnitude of this plot of the royal gang," his lordship said. "They had set out for world domination, these Kaisers and princes and princelings." Northcliffe made it clear that building ships and more ships was an urgent priority, to move troops and to move supplies to the allies on vessels that could outrun submarines. "War," he said, "is transport."

After the interview, Kirkwood gave the visitor a tour of the *Star*'s big brick headquarters, and for a few minutes they strode through the humming newsroom. "This morning Lord Northcliffe was in the office with his staff and Maj. General Leonard Wood too," Hemingway wrote, without elaboration, to his father. Hemingway surely noticed the Englishman's round, boyish face and perceived his aura of confidence. According to the newspaper's report of the Muehlebach luncheon, Northcliffe stood up for the foundation of journalism and spoke about its fearless pursuit of truth. Northcliffe had been criticized for his papers' insistence on giving equal weight to British losses and successes in the war, but he maintained that newspapers should not shy away from printing the truth. "I saw the only way for a democracy to fight was for the democracy to know the truth," he told the two hundred gathered newsmen. "The people ought to know the facts. That is the most certain way to arouse them to thorough participation in this war."

Breaking war news consumed much of the front page acreage of the *Star* and *Times*. Burris Jenkins's reporting on Europe was woven prominently into the coverage, his columns generally appearing inside the paper. In late October, Jenkins offered a depiction of the battle lines near Trieste in the first of a series of his accounts exploring the Italian front. "Everybody that knows Italy loves Italy," he wrote. The column gave a picture of what was just about to be lost: "You have but to see the swarming millions of soldiers back of her front and watch the smooth working of her machinery of supply and the incalculable industry of her road building, to awake to the fact that here is a noble and puissant people, rousing itself like a strong man." Jenkins considered the Italian front to be "the most dramatic, the most spectacular battle line in Europe." Hemingway's first glimpses of the Italian war would have come from these armchair travels with Jenkins:

The Alps lift the whole line up and hang it in festoons over their shoulders. You can look down upon the evening's guns, watch their fire, trace their projectiles, hear and see them fall and explode. You can stand behind your own guns and see the effect of your fire on a spot four miles away which, through the clear air, seems only half a mile.

You can see a whole battle field tilted up on edge, hung like a picture on the wall. You can walk from peak to peak, or ride, and examine the field from different angles. You can look down beneath at the gorges where wind the silver mountain rivers, with their pontoons yet bloody from recent daring conquests. You can look face to face upon mountain precipices, upon which Alpini have scaled like mountain goats, rifles strapped on shoulders and knives in teeth, in the fashion of the old days of chivalry.   .

Something of the sordid muddiness and undiluted industrialism of modern war here gives way to the romantic, dramatic spectacular. It is thrilling.

Jenkins's occasionally baroque vocabulary aside, his observations and reporting skills set a standard for readers of the *Star*. Twenty years later, in a memoir, Jenkins summed up his experience as a journalist in ways that Hemingway also understood. "I remained equally convinced of the value of newspaper training for a man who planned a career involving writing or public speaking. Such experience brings knowledge of humanity more rapidly than perhaps any other type of work," he wrote, echoing Richard Harding Davis's assessment of the reporting life. "It imparts brevity, conciseness, pungency of station, together with respect for facts, facts, facts, so essential to most forms of writing and speaking. Further, it gives one's style concreteness, vividness. It teaches one to 'talk in pictures' as Beecher described that trait."

Hemingway not much later developed his own version of the idea of talking in pictures by acknowledging the influence of painters on his writing. He learned to write as Cézanne painted, he'd say. (Jenkins himself, with his "battle field tilted up on edge, hung like a picture on the wall," brings Cézanne's tilted planes to mind.) In an interview with George Plimpton, Hemingway once listed his literary forebears, and along with Twain, Flaubert, and Stendhal, he tossed in Tintoretto, Hieronymus Bosch, Goya, and Van Gogh.

On October 25, 1917, the news from Europe did not look good for "the most spectacular battle line in Europe." On the day of Lord Northcliffe's visit to Kansas City, the Austro-German army breached Italian positions on the Isonzo front and took some ten thousand Italian prisoners. The Italians put up a fight on the western slope of Mont Santo Gabriel, but German artillery and infantry overpowered them almost everywhere else nearby. Hemingway followed the bulletins as they moved on the teletype machines and landed on the front pages of the *Times* and the *Star*. The Italians were preparing to evacuate the Bainsizza Plateau. The "northern wing of the second Italian army has been defeated and is retiring," read one item. Would Italy's cabinet resign? Despite the debacle, British observers remained hopeful that Italian munitions and troops would hold out and eventually reverse the German offensive. Another way to read the predominantly German campaign was as "further evidence of Austria's military impotence." Austria undoubtedly would remain under Berlin's thumb, according to informed observers.

––––––––––––––

At the end of his first week in Kansas City, Hemingway would have seen a feature story in his newspaper, credited to the *Detroit News*, that gave another, more personal perspective of the war in Italy. The story profiled a European nurse, the Countess Mazzuchi, who headed the war hospitals in Italy. She was in the United States on a fundraising tour, and to drum up support she brought mesmerizing tales of courage, adventure, danger, and healing.

"Blue fire flashes from the eyes of the Countess Mazzuchi," the story began, "angel of the Marne and valiant friend of the soldiers on the Italian firing line, as she tells of what her 'children' are enduring 'over there.'" The thirty-year-old countess was the daughter of a Spanish ambassador and an English woman. Her uncle was a cardinal. The story described her as girlish and attractive. Her husband served as the Italian consul general in the Marne district of France. Their chateau "has 5,000 shell holes in it today and her jewels have all been sold." She directed the proceeds of those sales to benefit Belgian and French soldiers, then to supply the chain of twenty-seven hospitals the countess managed for Italy's Third Army.

Countess Mazzuchi was fearless. She carried a bullet in her body, a wound she took in the battle of the Marne. She had been treating a young man, picking shrapnel out of his leg, and she didn't even notice she'd been shot. "I had two hundred wounded about me," she said. "Do you know that I was so intensely absorbed in what I was doing that I didn't even know I had a dirty German bullet in me until I tried to get up?" The countess was wounded again in Italy, amid a bout of heavy shelling, and she said her hacking cough was the result of "gas." The story included a long description of her work and quoted her extensively. "I was racing along when a bomb struck my bicycle and I was blown up and thrown forty meters back. My ribs were broken, but I quickly got to the hospital."

Hemingway, like most readers, would have been riveted by the countess's tale. She carried a bullet in her body. She was blown up at the Italian front. She was made a second lieutenant for her bravery and her wounds. The boy she was attending to in the Marne had 122 pieces of shrapnel in his leg. How common was that? What would that feel like? With all her qualities and experience under fire, the Countess Mazzuchi could be seen as a proto-version of Catherine Barkley, Frederic Henry, Nick Adams, and Hemingway himself rolled into one.

Lovely and heroic war nurses aside, at this point in his young career Hemingway was not yet totally consumed with the war in Europe. He was chasing more pedestrian assignments. Typical was a report on a three-year-old boy who died of rabies at General Hospital, having been bitten in the face by a dog, or the color paragraphs added to the coverage of a Liberty Loan Day parade, which attracted thirty-five thousand participants and passed by the *Star* building on its Grand Avenue route: "Although the procession was a notable spectacle, the throngs of spectators which lined the curbs, congested the sidewalks, filled stairways and occupied opened windows many stories from the street likewise made an interesting sight. It was a patriotic crowd, but some groups were more demonstrative than others. Many carried flags, which they waved frantically while a particularly attractive division of the column was passing."

While that sample reflects a descriptive simplicity, a routine effort by a cub reporter, the next, part of an item on the same page, appears to come from a more seasoned and glib observer, one capable of employing metaphor and thus providing a lesson in creativity that a young journalist could appreciate:

It was a jolly crowd that filled the streets after the parade yesterday afternoon. It smiled when it was bumped and it laughed when it was trampled on. The sense of duty it involved, a feeling of a part in the world's business made it so. It was the same spirit that Kansas City always goes in neck deep. A big job, one that made Kansas City show its teeth and grit them close together, as close as fight itself. It always has—and it always will as long as there is freedom to fight for. Before this Kansas City has done much, but yesterday she outdid herself.

If she has been awake before she is now not only awake, but out of bed. She showed it with her thousands marching.

As an obituary writer, Hemingway picked up on the unfortunate death of a city employee who collapsed while marching two blocks from the *Star* and died of heart disease. As the news item noticed, Amos R. Cecil did not let his age—sixty-two—"deter him from marching with the city hall delegation."

Hemingway boasted to his sister Marcelline that he'd had "six items in the sheet" that day. Besides the parade pieces, Hemingway likely produced a police item that served as another obituary, a story of a railroad laborer struck and killed by a Missouri Pacific engine in a train yard off Southwest Boulevard.

But still the foreign news rippled. The *Star* published maps of the action, ripe for studying the geography of northeastern Italy and absorbing the names of Italian places such as Gorizia and Udine. There is little doubt that the news stories from the Italian front helped feed Hemingway's rising hunger to join the action. By early November Hemingway was telling Marcelline that he intended to enlist in the Canadian Army. "Believe me," he wrote to her, "I will go not because of any love of gold braid glory etc. but because I couldn't face any body after the war and not have been in it."

In his travels to Italy, Burris Jenkins had come to the conclusion that American troops were desperately needed to stem the enemy's surge. So far, the American effort was mostly focused in France. On the eve of the Caporetto disaster, Jenkins remained optimistic:

One is overpowered by the thought that here, on the Italian front, is, after all, the weak spot in the Central Empire's defenses. Here concentration of allied artillery and airplanes would turn the trick, smash through, break quietly like a mountain torrent out of the mountains, upon the plateaus, run away to Vienna and cut the Central confederacy in two. This may be an amateur's estimate, but it is backed up by much good expert opinion.

The Italians have men enough; they need only guns and munitions. There must be reasons, in the jealous councils of the powers, otherwise this wedge would surely have been driven. Maybe America can lend a hand, if not in driving it, at least in promoting a more unified spirit among the Allies.

By early December, the *Star* would report that American aid to the Italian front was not far off. Much later, Hemingway would visit Jenkins's point in "A Way You'll Never Be," one of the Italian war stories that emanated from his own experience. Nicholas Adams wears an American uniform. He serves as a harbinger, meant to raise the spirits of the Italian soldiers. "If they see one American uniform," he tells an Italian battalion commander, "that is supposed to make them believe others are coming." Later Nick says there'll be "untold millions wearing this uniform swarming like locusts."

At the beginning of "Now I Lay Me," another of Hemingway's Italian stories, Nick is restless: "That night we lay on the floor in the room and I listened to the silkworms eating. The silkworms fed in racks of mulberry leaves and all night you could hear them eating and a dropping sound in the leaves." During his own Italian experience, Hemingway heard about that silkworm sound from Bill Horne, a friend he made in the ambulance service, who described hearing the very thing in his barracks. Burris Jenkins too observed "the mulberry trees, great orchards of them, Edens for the silkworm, who is pampered and nurtured, cared for as sedulously as if he were of royal blood; and royal is his product of Italian silk." Jenkins doesn't mention the feeding sound of silk-worms, but perhaps he gave Hemingway another sensory experience of Italy to pack away and recall when he needed it.

Burris Jenkins republished his *Star* dispatches in a book, *Facing the Hindenburg Line*, which arrived on store shelves by the end of 1917. His preface carried a cautionary note: "No man can come into close contact with this world misfortune and, if he have any imagination or any soul, come away with egoism accentuated. When many of the choicest men of earth: artists, scholars, musicians, men of letters, are dying—common soldiers in trenches—one can only feel the insignificance of self."

An eighteen-year-old high school graduate who had not yet discovered for himself the brutality of war might well have been inspired by Jenkins's sentiment. When, a decade later, that young man inspected and refracted what had happened to him on the Italian front, he could think again about the soul of a man, about egoism, and about his relative insignificance in a time of war.

Hemingway pushed open the oversized wooden front doors of the newspaper office and strode toward Eighteenth Street. After two blocks, at a slight incline, he rounded the corner south on Baltimore to Nineteenth Street. Police Station No. 4 occupied a two-story flatiron structure built in a Spanish-influenced style. It had opened just the previous year, completing a merger of the former station on Fifteenth Street and one off Southwest Boulevard. The station shared space with the South Side municipal court. It was a bit chilly outside and rain threatened, but back indoors the cub reporter sifted through police reports, called a rewrite man to file a few items by phone, and near the end of the day sat at a typewriter to compose a letter to his father. He rolled in a sheet of the police department's daily bulletin—*look out for a missing cow, nine lost and stolen cars, one Harley Davidson motorcycle found*—to compose his thoughts on the blank side. Among other things, he answered his father's inquiry about Carl Edgar. "He is 28 and is running the California Oil Burner Co.," Hemingway wrote. "He is a peach of a fellow and is a good pal of Bill Smith's."

Hemingway let on that as a newspaperman for all of one week, he'd already made his mark and got a bead on the effort to mobilize for war. He'd landed a scoop about the movement of troops to Camp Doniphan down in Oklahoma. He'd somehow worked his way past a barrier and talked with a captain who gave him "all the dope," though officially he wasn't supposed to say anything. Don't spread it around, he told his father. "I promised him I wouldnt publish it until the train had gone so it was OK." Hemingway the insider. For a novice reporter, it must have felt enlivening, an ego-builder. "In truth," Hemingway wrote to his sister the next day, "it is the life at this place."

Leicester Hemingway captured the flavor of his older brother's enthusiasm much later in a memoir, when he quoted Ernest: "I hit it lucky, because the people there liked to see young guys get out and deliver. Things broke my way quickly, like in a ball game."

5

A LACK OF VICES

I havnt seen a girl in Kansas City yet and that is a hard predicament
for a guy that has been in love with someone
ever since he can remember.
—Hemingway to his mother

Theodore Brumback, the suavely mustached son of a prominent Kansas City judge, noticed that the young reporter's
typewriter keys were sticking. "That's rotten looking copy," the
typist told him. "When I get a little excited this damn type mill
goes haywire on me." The young man at the keyboard stood up:
"My name's Hemingway."

Brumback recalled that greeting almost twenty years later in
an article he wrote for the *Star*. It was 1936, and Ernest Hemingway, author of *The Sun Also Rises* and *A Farewell to Arms*,
had become a household name. His travel memoir *Green Hills
of Africa*, an experimental book about hunting and writing, had
come out the year before (although to some vicious reviews),
and Hemingway's byline appeared regularly in magazines. Just
recently *Esquire* had published "The Snows of Kilimanjaro," a
notable piece of short fiction also inspired by the African journey,

and *Cosmopolitan* introduced readers to "The Short Happy Life of Francis Macomber," again with its setting on a hunt. Brumback had just returned to Kansas City from a long stretch in California, where he worked in real estate. He took an opportunity to remember the Hemingway he knew at the *Kansas City Star* and in the war zone in Italy. They had traveled there together to serve in the Red Cross ambulance service in the spring of 1918. Brumback's story was quite entertaining and revealing of Hemingway's bold sense of adventure, but part of it, repeated endlessly by later Hemingway biographers, was wrong.

Brumback suggested that his meeting with Hemingway over the stuck typewriter keys occurred when he, Brumback, joined the newspaper's staff. ("You're a new man, aren't you?" Hemingway says in Brumback's story.) But *Star* colleague Dale Wilson later recalled that Hemingway's first encounter with Brumback occurred when Brumback showed up in the *Star*'s newsroom one Saturday in mid-November 1917. Hemingway was assigned to interview him.

Brumback had just returned to his hometown from a five-month stint driving American Field Service ambulances in France. Brumback, like Hemingway, had been rejected from military service because of an eye problem. He'd lost one of his in a rude encounter with a golf ball while attending Cornell University. He enlisted for ambulance duty in July 1917, just a few months after the United States declared its intention to join the war in Europe. Back in August, the *Star* had published a letter Brumback had written to his father, Jackson County circuit judge Hermann Brumback, about a night in July when "the Germans tried to cut off all communication by a most frightful bombardment." Brumback added, "A French lieutenant told me that even at Verdun he had never seen so many 'marmites' fall behind the lines."

Now, in November, the *Star* found it fitting to announce Brumback's return, ostensibly on a month's furlough. The story reported, however, that Brumback was "disqualified from further service in the ambulance section, which now have been taken over by the government." According to the story, Brumback's section No. 66 was situated in back of the Craonne sector, which the August letter had described as "one of the hottest fighting districts along the front. Troops of the German crown prince were opposite."

Brumback gave the reporter—most likely Hemingway—a quick picture of what the service entailed. "There are three thousand Americans in the ambulance service," Brumback said. "The forty-four men in our section one day brought back fifteen hundred wounded men. We were seldom that busy, however, and sometimes for a day or two we would have practically no work."

The reporter paraphrased the rest: The ambulance headquarters operated on the Aisne River, about four miles back of the line but easily within gun range. Wounded men were hauled in motor ambulances about five miles, where other ambulances picked them up and carried them to base hospitals. In quiet times ambulance drivers worked two days at the front, then spent four days in the rear. During an attack they worked continuously. The brief story concluded by noting the souvenirs Brumback brought with him to the *Star* for display: "a hand grenade, a trench bomb and several pieces of shrapnel, one of which fell in his ambulance." The bomb was seven inches long and would have weighed about two pounds when filled, making for an easy toss by a soldier aiming for the enemy. Two days later, the paper followed up the Brumback story with linecut images of the young man and his souvenir trench bomb.

The *Star* illustrated Ted Brumback's return to Kansas City with a portrait of him in uniform and the trench bomb he'd brought back from France. *Kansas City Star*

It remains unclear when Brumback joined the newspaper staff. A few days after the story about his return appeared, Brumback gave a luncheon talk about his service to the Real Estate Board. "On an ordinary night it was all very well," Brumback told his audience at the Coates House Hotel, "but it was a different thing when overhead one heard the purr of a Gotha motor or the sharp, staccato bark of a machine gun." A *Star* story about that event identified Brumback as an associate member of the group and said he had worked for the J. C. Nichols Co., a leading real estate developer, before he went to France. There was no mention of Brumback as a *Star* reporter. Nor did another story in December, announcing a Brumback talk at a church, mention an association with the newspaper. The story about his lecture at the Real Estate Board luncheon, however, gave further details of the young man's service. It quoted him at length, about the sound of shells, the need for American support, and the ravaged French countryside: "Most of the towns I have passed through have been literally razed to the ground. So many unexploded shells lie about the fields, that to my mind, it will be a great problem after the war to till the soil."

Brumback's speech rounded out the narratives of war that Burris Jenkins had been writing. He brought a personal perspective of action on the front. If Hemingway didn't write this story, too, he surely read it, and at some point soon an important friendship began and an idea about both young men's futures would be hatched.

Months before Hemingway joined the ambulance service in Italy, he took a professional interest in the ambulances of Kansas City, which at that moment were having troubles. AMBULANCE SERVICE IS BAD AND THE PHYSICIANS REBEL, read a *Star* headline in early November. The story introduced a conflict in the city's health bureaucracy and the General Hospital that would occupy Hemingway's reporting time for much of his stint at the *Star*. In short, doctors were underpaid and overworked, and hospitals were short staffed. Three of six city physicians had been assigned as ambulance surgeons, and doctors were threatening to quit. They made $75 a month, the same as the drivers, and the same, for that matter, as Hemingway would soon be earning after his first month's probation was complete at the *Star*. The doctors wanted $125, and they wanted another ambulance surgeon on staff. Interns tried to fill in, contrary to hospital policy, but one had been punished recently, his pay withheld for going out on a call. A brief rebellion ensued, and interns continued to break the rule when their help was needed. On a recent Saturday, for example, "Two calls were received, one to get a man who had cut his throat in attempted suicide, the other for a man in whose arm an artery had been severed. The calls came about five minutes apart. No doctors were in the receiving ward to make the calls. Fully fifteen minutes after the calls were received two internes went out only because of the nature of the cases, and they broke a rule in going." Dr. E. W. Washburn, General Hospital's business manager, said money was tight and nothing could be done until April. Hemingway had an affinity for the world of medical practice. His father's occupation exposed the young boy to the surgeon's milieu and the science of health. In the coming months, Hemingway would get to know some of those ambulance surgeons quite well, and the hospital's emergency room and Washburn, too, would loom large in his reporting and writing experience.

The tug of military service was persistent. As Americans trained, as the war raged on, as the *Star* reported on young men from the region who died on the battlefield, and as the drumbeat for action and heroism got louder, Hemingway couldn't help but visualize a role for himself. In early November, his reporting assignments and personal encounters fed his evolving plans. That idea about joining the Canadians was real, "but," he told Marcelline, "may wait till spring brings back Blue days and Fair." Hemingway, as usual, was showing off, alluding in that phrase to a line of poetry from Alan Seeger's "I Have a Rendezvous with Death." The poem had been published just that year. Seeger had joined the French Foreign Legion earlier in the war and was killed in the Battle of the Somme in 1916. Fate and duty and heroism swirled in the young Hemingway's head. He told Marcelline he was anxious about getting into the action. Hemingway boasted that he had befriended officers in charge of the Canadian Mission in Kansas City, so he had picked up some useful guidance. Enlisting in Canadian forces meant you could join whenever you wanted to, travel through London, and end up in France within three months. He also picked up a feeling of Canadian pride: "They are the greatest fighters in the world and our troops are not to be spoken of in the same breath."

Hemingway seemed to be channeling the enthusiasm of Capt. R. W. Simmie, whom he name-dropped in the letter to Marcelline. Simmie ran the British mission in Kansas City, at 901 Main Street, though clearly he represented the Canadian branch of the military. "The Canadians are great prowlers," Simmie told a *Star* reporter, probably Hemingway, "and they rather creep forward. They are the best trench raiders in the game." Simmie's story was inspiring enough for a return engagement. In December, the newspaper carried an account of his heroism and near-death experience during a battle against Germans in October 1916 at Courcelette, France. Simmie suffered shrapnel wounds in his legs while meeting German attacks for eight hours in the trenches. His company lost many men, and he was one of only five who survived, but they'd killed many Germans and had taken scores of prisoners. Simmie was awarded the military cross for conspicuous gallantry and promoted to captain. Accompanying the story was a portrait and an image of the cross.

Hemingway knew that his namesake grandfather, Ernest Hall, had been wounded not far away, in Butler, Missouri, fighting for the Union in the Civil War. Hemingway made an effort to follow in his grandfather's footsteps when he joined the Missouri Guard, a home militia that had been inaugurated in August after the previous National Guard unit had been designated for service in France. As he wrote to Marcelline, he had a uniform (forty dollars) and an overcoat (fifty dollars): "Some youth." The guard armory stood at Thirty-Ninth and Main, just a few blocks from Hemingway's uncle's house and Miss Haynes's boardinghouse. On November 13, Hemingway joined about 750 guardsmen for a training day at Swope Park. The vast expanse of lawn and woods on the southeast edge of the city provided varied settings for skirmishes, raids, and other maneuvers. One battle involved possession of a railroad bridge and "would have been bloody if the guns hadn't been all wood." A couple days later, Hemingway told his parents that the daylong maneuvers were "very thrilling and instructive too."

Despite Hemingway's exposure to the guard service and khakis, he remained unsure of what he wanted to do and when. To his parents, he said he'd work till spring, plan another "good summer"—a Michigan vacation, that is—before enlisting.

At eighteen, Hemingway had an outdoorsman's stride, a tanned face, and a widow's-peak hairline. His quiet but engaging manner made him approachable, and he relished absorbing whatever wisdom he could from the older journalists around him. To hear the accounts of some of his Kansas City contemporaries, the young Hemingway came under the spell of an older, wilder itinerant reporter named Lionel Calhoun Moise. At the time Hemingway arrived, Moise apparently was making his second appearance at the *Star*, expanding his legend as an accomplished writer and prodigious drinker. "He is preserved in the minds of his contemporaries as a symbol of a vanished species," Fenton writes, "the boomer, the nomad reporter who acknowledged no master, moving turbulently from job to job, able neither to write a dull story nor be a dull companion. He was notorious as a cop-slugger and barroom brawler." For his study in the early 1950s of Hemingway's apprenticeship, Charles A. Fenton collected testimony from several *Star* staffers who placed the gullible cub at the feet of Moise and his mastery. Hemingway was "an apt and industrious pupil," and he and Moise "became good friends," Fenton concluded. Moise himself recounted that Hemingway "accorded me the deferential attention of a mere cub listening to the priceless wisdom of a veteran *Star* man who'd also labored—such distinction!—on the Chi Trib, N.Y. World, S.F. Bulletin, etc. etc."

Hemingway, in letters to the Yale scholar, rejected Fenton's emphasis on Moise, told him it was all out of proportion, and warned that he'd been listening to the wrong people. Of all the newsmen and friends Fenton had tracked down, he missed "at least ten men on the Star who were better friends of mine than Lionel Moise." Fenton had heard a similar warning from Elizabeth Moffett, the *Star*'s woman's editor and "Mother Moffett" to Hemingway. "It sort of irks me to have anyone think Moise helped shape his career," she told Fenton. "As I remember he had no importance on the *Star*."

Clearly Hemingway was not a fan of the legend:

I knew Moise only slightly and what impressed me most in him was his facility, his un-disciplined talent and his enormous vitality which when he was drinking, and I never saw him when he was not drinking, over-flowed into violence. I never, to my knowledge, heard him discuss writing seriously. His style of journalism as I recall it at that time was flamboyant and rhetorical and what amazed me was the facility with which he turned it out. I saw very little of him because we worked in different parts of town. I always spoke well of him and always will. But I was appalled by the way he wasted his talent and by his violence.

Fenton interviewed Carl Edgar about Moise, but Hemingway also dismissed that. He was sure that Edgar never met him. Edgar never met many of "the other characters" from the *Star* with whom Hemingway went around town. "You were working on Kansas City and missed all of them," Hemingway told Fenton. Even Pete Wellington, Hemingway's immediate boss, would not have kept track of his life outside the office. They weren't friends at all. Later in his letter, more like a diatribe, Hemingway relents and tells Fenton to go ahead and use the stuff from Moise because it would make the old man feel good and he wanted to please Moise and Wellington.

The documentary evidence is slight, but one extant scrap of paper at the *Star* appears to favor Hemingway's version of the Moise story. If Hemingway spent any time at all with Moise, the mentorship didn't last very long. By November 5, barely three weeks after Hemingway's apprenticeship began, Moise's name was excised from the newspaper's payroll and he was on his way to another stop on his raucous trail.

Hemingway once sketched a quick profile of Moise, scratching it out on three sheets of telegram paper. All these years later, we cannot be certain if he were aiming for accuracy or imagining a work of fiction: "Lionel Moise was a great re-write man," Hemingway wrote. "He could carry four stories in his head and go to the telephone and take a fifth and then write all five at full speed to catch an edition. There would be something alive about each one. . . . He never spoke to the other reporters unless he had been drinking. He was tall and thick and had long arms and big hands. He was the fastest man on a typewriter I ever knew. He drove a motor car and it was understood in the office that a woman had given it to him. One night she stabbed him in it out on the Lincoln Highway half way to Jefferson City. He took the knife away from her . . . and threw it out of the car. Then he did something awful to her. She was lying in the back of the car when they found them. Moise drove the car all the way into Kansas City with her fixed that way."

At some point Moise, possibly in 1918, ended up in New York, where he eventually conducted a tempestuous relationship with Dorothy Day and furthered his reputation as a cad. Day, the future novelist, was in nursing school, and Moise was working as a hospital orderly, according to one account. And drinking heavily. Moise got Day pregnant and bullied her into having an abortion. The poet Kenneth Rexroth, a onetime cub reporter in Chicago, encountered the Moise legend in passing and remembered him in exceptionally colorful terms:

> There was a group of girls who were almost all prostitutes who had drifted in off North Clark Street, lonely for coffee and company. . . . One was the girl of Lionel Moise, pronounced Mo-ees, the man who is supposed to have taught Ernest Hemingway how to write. At least she was one of what whores call his wives-in-law, and shared him with a newspaper woman, a sculptress, and the daughter of a millionaire judge. Saturday nights, when the girls got drunk on Bugs Moran's gin, the battles over the beautiful, beloved body of Lionel Moise were epical. . . . None of these people was a fool or a hoodlum. All the girls were beautiful; even the one who went by the name of Sloppy Liz was fairly good-looking, and they all made devoted mistresses, wives, and nurses for husbands, who were always being put in jail or beaten up for alcoholism or Revolution, or both. Lionel Moise had sound ideas about good writing, ideas of which Hemingway's Marquis of Queensbury esthetics are only a caricature.

Hemingway's combative aesthetics, his desire to pummel the likes of Tolstoy and Dostoevsky, lay somewhat in the future. As for women, Moise's reputation might have been a cautionary tale, but Hemingway undoubtedly got a Kansas City education in solicitous streetwalkers, courtesy of the police and hospital beats. Yet after a month at the *Star* he lamented to his mother that "I havnt seen a girl in Kansas City yet and that is a hard predicament for a guy that has been in love with someone ever since he can remember." For recreation, Hemingway and his best pal Carl Edgar made weekend excursions to Edgar's hometown, St. Joseph. One night in early November they went out on the town in Kansas City and went to the Shubert Theater to see *Turn to the Right!*, a recent Broadway production now on the road. Winchell Smith and John Hazzard's comedy involved a young man from the country who overcomes an unjust prison sentence, does a good deed, and wins the heart of a swindling deacon's daughter. Hemingway admitted to Marcelline that the "debasing theater" was one of his only vices.

6

THE "GREAT LITTERATEUR"

I read only the newspaper and lyric poetry.
The papers contain life and the poems truth.
—Knut Hamsun

Hemingway's training in literature, the fire fanned by Fannie Biggs and other teachers at Oak Park and River Forest High School, continued daily in the *Star's* newsroom. The ambitious readers and writers on the exchange desk provided a substitute for the college English classes Hemingway had put off that year. They peppered the newspaper's pages with literary news, book excerpts, and a general sense of cultural conversation. A regional novel, *Keith of the Border: A Tale of the Plains*, by Randall Parrish, got the serial treatment on the op-ed pages that fall, putting readers in the not-too-distant history of the West. On a lighter note, the exchange editors often recycled excerpts from one of Hemingway's favorite reads, the B.L.T. column in the *Chicago Tribune*. As one item explained: "The man from Chicago suddenly ceased to laugh. 'Excuse me a moment,' he said. 'I must write that down and send it in to B.L.T.' When a Chicagoan makes a pun or cracks a joke or runs across a piece of unconscious humor in the semi-rural press he sends it on to Bert Leston Taylor for his daily columns of humor in the Chicago Tribune." The story went on for another half column, quoting a day's worth of Taylor's witticisms. Hemingway, deemed the cleverest boy in his high school, loved it. He'd asked his father to send along some of B.L.T's A Line o' Type or Two columns and was pleased to find them in the mail one day.

Perhaps more instructive to Hemingway's developing identity as a writer was the *Star's* prominent excerpt of an interview with the Norwegian writer Knut Hamsun. It was a little seminar in print, which originated with the *New York Evening Post.* Hamsun had not yet won the Nobel Prize in Literature—that would happen in 1920—but he was sufficiently well known to merit attention from Hemingway's bookish colleagues. Hamsun, the piece noted, had once worked as a streetcar conductor in Chicago, part of an American sojourn that soured the Norwegian's view of the states. Yet Hamsun delivered some ponderable thoughts on writing. "I read only the newspaper and lyric poetry," he said. "The papers contain life and the poems truth." The interviewer went on to ask whether Hamsun based his characters on "living models":

"Not at all. I never used a living model but once and that work was not successful. I never know at the beginning how my characters are going to come out; what is going to become of them. I start them, add a little each day, and at the close they stand before me generally in a way which I myself never anticipated. Life has its own rules and these rules determine the fate of my characters."

"Then you do not have and do not believe in a theory of composition?"

"None other than the one I have just stated. The biggest bit of balderdash that was ever written is Poe's account of his composition of 'The Raven.' While writing a novel or drama I make it a point to read much poetry in the meantime. That stimulates. Also, in the evening, while sitting in as near total darkness as possible, I take down notes. The next morning I make use of as many of these as I can. Sometimes I can use all of them, sometimes very few."

It's not hard to imagine Hemingway at some point sitting in "near total darkness" to consult his stimulated brain for poetic inspiration. Years later in Paris, as he wrote in *A Moveable Feast*, he'd squeeze an orange peel into a fire to see blue sparks as he searched for a "true sentence." And he did once test Ted Brumback's patience and his sleep with an extended late-night reading of Robert Browning. But moments of insight clearly clicked from time to time in Kansas City, epiphanies and episodes that Hemingway held onto and found useful as he chiseled his writing self in subsequent years.

One of those episodes occurred late on a November night. A trio of thieves, "Cap" Gargotta, Joe Musso, and an accomplice, had broken into the Parker-Gordon Cigar Co. at 1028 Broadway and hauled away a load of cigars and tobacco. Police detectives Jack Farrell and Carl Grantello encountered the robbers and chased them eastward, then north on Main Street. Farrell pulled his gun and fatally shot Gargotta and Musso in what appeared to be an act of overzealous policing. The detectives captured a third robber, F. P. Jennings. These sketchy details appeared in a brief, four-paragraph news item on the front page of the morning paper. When Hemingway arrived at work that Monday morning he found his name penciled in on the assignment sheet to follow up the news with police.

The material he gathered for the afternoon edition fleshed out the story. Among other things it corrected the two dead robbers' names, which had been misspelled in the deadline brief filed after midnight. But the afternoon story quoted the survivor, who described the crime and confessed that his only participation was to drive the getaway vehicle, a covered wagon. "I met 'Cap' Gargotta at Fifth Street and Grand Avenue last night," Jennings told a detective, "and he asked me if I wanted to make some money." The thieves made off with tobacco goods valued at about $3,000, and as police approached, near Third and Main, Jennings, Gargotta, and Musso aimed their horses right at them. In reporting the story Hemingway learned the suspects were part of a crime syndicate responsible for a recent rash of downtown business robberies.

Despite having worked on the longer story that day, Hemingway clearly found something compelling about the original news item in the morning edition. It's quite possible he had written it. He typically took Sundays off, but not always, and he liked the action and often worked when he wasn't regularly scheduled, even late into the night, as the breaking news story would have required. In Paris, five years later, Hemingway transformed that first news item into a work of fiction. For his own purposes, Hemingway pulled apart each sentence of the news story and reinvented it with new names and other details. It became a compact vignette included in his first book of fiction, the Paris-published *in our time*, which he later expanded and republished in the United States as *In Our Time* (1925).

In the fictional version, the perpetrators were not of Italian heritage but Hungarian, suggesting a reflection on Hemingway's wartime friends and enemies. He gave the police officers fictional names as well, though he picked two names, Drevitts and Boyle, that belonged to two actual Kansas City detectives he must have

POLICE KILL TWO IN CHASE.

Third Cigar Store Robber Was Caught
by Detectives!

Two thieves, found carting a quantity
of cigars and tobacco away from the
Parker-Gordon Cigar Company's building, 1028 Broadway, shortly after midnight, were shot and killed by police
in the chase that followed.

Jack Farrell and Carl Grantello were
the detectives who discovered the
thieves at work and who fired at the
men as they fled east to Main Street
and north toward the city hall. A third
robber was captured.

F. P. Jennings was the man who was
captured. The men who were killed
were shot in the head.

The police identified the dead men as
"Cap" Gargetto and Joe Muco.

Late on a Sunday night in November 1917, a crime story broke in
time to make the next morning's newspaper. Hemingway would remember it a few years later while writing the vignettes of the Paris
edition of *in our time*. *Kansas City Star*

known. As he drafted the story, he toyed with titles and seemed
to want to call it "Crime and Punishment." That was a nod, of
course, to Dostoyevsky, whose influence on Hemingway would
become evident in the Kansas City newsroom soon enough, as
another crime story unfolded two months after the cigar store
robbers bled out in the nighttime street.

———————

Hemingway developed a fascination with the many older men
who worked around him at the *Star*. He was quick to develop
nicknames for some of them. Along with the pop-eyed Smith the
Beamer, there was "Lackpants" Hicks, so named for his threadbare

clothes. He was often shy and reserved around his elders, but his inner jester was never far away. Todd Ormiston, who had a racy reputation with women, was the "White Slaver," according to Dale Wilson, and William Moorhead, who covered police headquarters, was "Broken Bill," for his bad luck around the poker table. Hemingway got his buddies to call him Hemingstein, if not "the great Hemingstein." To his siblings he was "the great litterateur Stien" (he meant Stein). Elizabeth Moffett, the woman's editor who presided over society writers and assistants on the building's first floor, was "Mother" Moffett to all, and she turned the tables on him by anointing him "Hemmy."

Over time and through close observation, Hemingway made deeper judgments about some of the characters who scratched and sweated around him in the Kansas City news business. He sketched a devastating portrait of mediocrity in a short story, never published, that had roots in the Kansas City newsroom. The story involved one Morrow Alford, a veteran but undistinguished reporter of fifteen years. Alford, known as Punk, felt trapped by his unsatisfying job but found solace in gardening and imagining murder mysteries that he was never able to write. Punk Alford was no reporting superstar, Hemingway wrote; his was the stuff that never got read beginning to end.

That judgment—the best this man could do was not nearly good enough—is merciless. Hemingway's ego would fight against that kind of criticism for the rest of his life. But Punk Alford was not totally unaware of his limitations, nor was he wholly unable to spark a momentary flash of ambition. In this baroque and creaky story—it doesn't help that the eleven-page manuscript is missing one page in the middle—Punk Alford takes it upon himself to investigate a murder and ultimately confront the killer in a moralistic climax. Whether Hemingway based the character on any single real person is impossible to say. But, as with many

Hemingway stories, the characters and details contained grains of actuality. A man named Morrow Alford indeed worked at the *Star*, as did George Wallace, known as Punk. As Hemingway learned quite well at the newspaper, the art of fiction begins in the pulse and drama of real lives. Colonel Nelson championed stories of human interest above all. He knew that people understood people, and the everyday lives of people could be fodder for compelling newspaper stories. That guidance clearly could be useful to a writer with higher ambitions.

The creative writers at the *Star* found human drama all over town. And they had no compunction about dealing with the fact-and-fiction matter in print. One feature story even offered in its lead a sort of direct, metafictional address to readers, far ahead of its time: "Newspaper stories have to have headlines and they have to have facts. If this one lacked the headlines you'd never guess how it was coming out. If it were fiction, the editor would kill it. And if this manner of telling plays bob with all the approved rules—why, so does the whole romance flout all the copybook maxims."

At this point the narrative unfolds: Miss Eula Bishop drops her lunch on the way to work. A young man named Howard DeHart picks it up and begins quietly wooing her. She's a sales girl; he's a ribbon clerk somewhere else. She thinks him too timid to take him seriously, so he tries to pump up his manly résumé by confessing to a series of holdups. He walks her home every night. She tells a friend, who tells someone else, and then the guy's arrested. The cops, though, soon realize Howard is not a holdup man, and he says, aw shucks, I guess you don't want me anymore. Eula says she'll marry him. And her boss throws them a party and hires Howard to sell trousers.

Sometimes the drama involved the very writer of the story. If Hemingway had little direct experience with Lionel Moise, he had none with Courtney Ryley Cooper, who had departed the staff a few years earlier but remained a legend in the newsroom. Cooper was a near-mythological creature, possessing high energy and a rowdy reputation. At fifteen, he ran away from home to join the circus and become a clown. By the time he landed at the *Star*, in 1906, he was twenty, and he'd been a salesman, a press agent for Buffalo Bill, and a vaudeville dancer. Even as a rookie reporter he began to write so well that Nelson put him in charge of the exchange desk, where all of the newsroom's best writers worked. When Cooper began writing fiction after hours and earning a healthy stream of freelance income, Nelson lowered his beefy arms on his desk, told him that being a *Star* man was a twenty-four-hour-a-day job, and fired him (with no lasting hard feelings). Later Cooper gained some fame as a novelist, magazine writer, and publicist for J. Edgar Hoover of the FBI.

But in Hemingway's period at the *Star*, the newsroom's collective memory wouldn't soon forget a certain September night in 1910, back when the newspaper operated in a building at Eleventh and Grand. Shortly before ten o'clock, two men had attacked Cooper at Tenth and Central Streets as he walked from the Grand Theater to the Kansas City Athletic Club. They cut his throat with a knife and hit him over the head before fleeing. Police suspected Cooper was targeted because of a series of anticrime stories he'd been writing. The injuries turned out to be not serious, though the emergency room surgeon noted the knife had sliced flesh within an inch of Cooper's jugular. Bandaged and released, Cooper did what any committed newsman would do. After making a statement at police headquarters, he headed back to the office, lined up a sheaf of copy paper, picked up a soft-lead pencil, and wrote the story for the next day's edition. Other newsmen stood around and watched him in awe.

Cooper, in short, was no Punk Alford. He became a bona fide talent. Two decades later, Cooper recalled his Kansas City newspaper experience in the *Saturday Evening Post*. It was a vivid tribute to Nelson and his legacy. His beginner's experience with *Star* editors was very much like what Hemingway would face a decade later. At the time, Henry Haskell was Cooper's city editor. One day early on, Cooper was assigned to write up an obituary. After he turned in the three-sentence item, Haskell called Cooper to his desk. In full hearing of the rest of the staff, Haskell told him to remember how he wrote the story so he could check it against the published version a few hours later. Cooper returned to his desk.

> The afternoon edition came off the presses. I found my story deep inside and read it. Mr. Haskell was out of the room. I went to Mr. Dillon [Haskell's assistant].
>
> "How is this different?" I asked. As if he had expected the question, he reached to a corner of the desk for my original copy.
>
> "This is how it's different: In the first place, this piece of human flesh was all together, wasn't it?"
>
> "Oh, yes, sir."
>
> "Then it was the body of John Jones, not the remains. Again, you mentioned that this was John Jones, deceased."
>
> "Isn't that right?"
>
> "Legally, yes. Reportorially, no. Nobody ever deceases in this office. He dies. A funeral is a procession. Are they going to take horses into the undertaker's?"
>
> "No, sir."
>
> "Then there will be funeral services. The funeral follows. And persons will be present, not people. Regarding the usage

of A.M. and P.M., this is a newspaper and not a railroad timetable. And we never inter anybody. We bury."

Red-faced, shaky, I turned back to my desk. Everybody began to scribble again, except one man. He leaned across the schoolroom aisle to me and said:

"Don't mind that. The best of us get it."

———————

After he finished his work on the cigar store robbery story that Monday afternoon, Hemingway kept going until after six o'clock. Then he was overdue for a letter home, so he rolled a sheet of paper into the typewriter and started at it again. He told his parents how busy he'd been with work. He mentioned that he'd had Sunday dinner with his aunt and uncle. Before that, a barn had caught fire next door to their house, and he'd gotten there in time to help firefighters put it out and even lugged a hose up to the roof. He thanked his parents for sending postage stamps and cookies. He passed on greetings from friends and engaged in a few other items of small talk. He was happy to be among a "dandy bunch of fellows." They were having a jolly time pulling pranks on a new man. And one more thing, the doctor's son added: "I have ridden in the Ambulance several times and as there is an epidemic of small pox here I think I will get vacinated [sic] again tomorrow."

7

A SUICIDE, A FLEA, A VILE PLACE

*The spelling in this is not to be watshed as I am pounding
in a big hurry and not stopping to correct mistakes.*
—Hemingway to his parents

Kansas City had a drug problem. And booze. There was too much booze, and too much of it too easily available to the young men who were training to go off to war. And when booze was so easily available, loose women were not far away. Kansas City officials got a wakeup call when the secretary of war put Hemingway's new city on notice. "Numerous complaints have reached this department," Newton D. Baker told the mayor, "that liquor is being sold to soldiers and vice is easy of access to the military forces upon visiting Kansas City. May I rely upon your co-operation in securing and maintaining clean conditions in Kansas City?"

Mayor George Edwards read the telegram and quaked. He thought everything was under control. Just a week earlier he'd announced that vice was on the decline. He cornered Larry Ghent, the acting police chief. Ghent assured Edwards that police were "doing everything possible." Not good enough.

Ghent told Edwards that prostitutes were under pressure to get off the streets. He complained he couldn't do much about the bars. "As long as we have saloons here soldiers are going to get liquor." He said civilians never hesitated to buy a bottle for a soldier. And rooming houses, some of them more accurately described as "immoral resorts," seemed to be an uncontrollable source of free-flowing alcohol and other temptations. One municipal court judge of Hemingway's acquaintance fined a chauffeur $500 for selling liquor and drugs to soldiers in a Twelfth Street rooming house and scolded him, "Persons like you, who entice soldiers to whisky, drugs and women are a worse menace to the Nation's defense than the German army."

The War Department was threatening to make Kansas City off-limits to the soldiers training at Camp Funston. The chief of police and a police commissioner got what amounted to a dressing down when they visited with Secretary Baker in Washington. Baker "said if it were necessary a man should be stationed at the door of every such place to take the names of every man going in—that no effort must be spared to clean Kansas City up of vice conditions from which soldiers had suffered. Otherwise he made it plain a quarantine would be placed against the city."

Hemingway was getting the impression that Kansas City must be the mother lode of sin and bad behavior. A recent report had spread alarm about narcotics. The local public welfare board concluded Kansas City had the worst record of any city in violations of the Harrison antinarcotics law. Since December 1914, the Harrison Narcotics Tax Act had imposed taxes on opiates and coca-leaf products. The welfare board's president, H. R. Ennis, complained that the law was defective and enforcement efforts were understaffed. He tried to get that message across in Washington. Still, the report, based on a few recent weeks of research, found a persistent culture of narcotics distribution. "The report shows twenty-one physicians, ten drug stores and sixteen peddlers named by drug addicts as having written prescriptions for drugs or made sales," the *Star* said. "It was shown that peddlers visit certain sections at recognized hours, while some confine operations to particular locations."

Among 250 local addicts, including laborers, waiters, cooks, salesmen, chambermaids, musicians, and machinists, three were identified as physicians in the report's demographic data. Though incredible to some, that fact would have been little surprise to Hemingway. He later sketched out a scene, never published, about an ambulance surgeon in Kansas City with the habit. In the four-page, handwritten fragment of a story, Hemingway mentions the Harrison act and says Doc Kling was something of a maverick. The doctor laments the circumstances that push prostitutes and boxers and "the movie people" to use narcotics and then get hooked. The man knew what he was talking about. He rolled up a sleeve and showed the sketch's narrator the blue circles and dark puncture marks on his lower arm. They were talking in the hospital's receiving ward, and the narrator—the voice of the young Hemingway, that is—expresses his fear that someone would walk by and see the sorry sight.

Hemingway would revisit that image later. "A Pursuit Race," one of his two published short stories with a Kansas City setting, offered an eerie profile of addiction. William Campbell, an advance man for a burlesque show, is holed up in a hotel room, drunk and wigging out. The show's manager catches up to him. Campbell rolls up his sleeve to show him the problem. In an unpublished section of a draft of the story, Hemingway describes a similar blue and punctured landscape on Campbell's forearm.

Campbell tells the manager it's his new habit, backed up every now and then by drink to chase "the wolf" away.

That winter, the head of the welfare board issued another alarming report about rampant drug abuse in Kansas City. The Municipal Farm was housing one hundred addicts a day at great cost. Some city leaders listening to the speaker at a City Club meeting were hearing some of this for the first time and were "shocked and ashamed of their city." It was a "rotten, immoral, 'wide open' town," according to the *Star*'s story about the speech by H. R. Ennis, where corrupt doctors got young women hooked on narcotics and drugstores sold morphine, heroin, and cocaine openly and the cops and courts looked the other way. It was odd that city leaders seemed unaware. The *Star* had been reporting on the problem for months. The warnings about a government-imposed quarantine began arriving in early November. "Unless Kansas City puts a vice-tight lid on the immoral houses, the places selling liquor to the soldiers and the women who solicit on the street," the newspaper intoned, "Kansas City may suffer the humiliation of being put in a barred military zone. In addition the business men are faced with the possibility of losing thousands of dollars from sales to the soldiers coming here each week from Camp Funston, Fort Leavenworth and other military training camps." The police department's three vice squads got to work, raiding the odd rooming house from time to time, but the effort seemed mostly for show.

Hemingway's newspaper work exposed him not only to these urban scourges but also to small human dramas almost every day. On one early December swing through the vast Union Station, a regular stop on the daily assignment sheet, he got tipped to an evocative turn in a story that had been in the news in recent days. He was rather proud of it and sent a clipping to his parents.

A few minutes after a through train for California left the Union Station yesterday morning, an usher found this note on the track:

When this note is found I will be on the Santa Fe and the deed will be done. I have loved, but in vain, so I leave this world. Please notify Eva Frampton, 2210 the Paseo. She will know. Good-by; good luck; God bless you, is all I can say.

"*R.C.B.*"

The usher turned the note over to the police and a patrolman, sent to investigate, found a girl named Eva Frampton had lived there but had moved to the West View Hotel, 1016 Jefferson Street. It was later learned there had been no suicide on the train.

Miss Frampton was the complaining witness in the trial of W.C. Bowman for assault. Bowman was sentenced to the penitentiary for nine years. Yesterday in the supreme court at Jefferson City the judgment was reversed and the case remanded because of errors in the admission of testimony.

Last night Miss Frampton said that she believed that Bowman was the author of the note.

"The suicide note was a lot of fun," Hemingway told his parents the next day, "as I [got] to go and interview the girl in the case, and I had the regular police star that we keep here for emergencies, and so she told me everything she knew then I got a story the man Bowman, and had him give me samples of his handwriting and scared him pea green." If Hemingway really had put the scare into Bowman, a story reflecting his handwriting sample never made the paper. But other stories and an editorial further described Bowman's alleged crime. He and another man had encountered the teenaged Eva Frampton and a companion, had drinks in a saloon, and took them for a ride toward Independence. Along the way, the girls alleged, the men attacked them. Bowman's defense included his belief that Frampton was not fifteen but sixteen. The tale offered another dimension that Hemingway was beginning to recognize in the workings of Kansas City: the power and corruption of politics. Bowman was politically connected, and his prosecution had stumbled through repeated procedural obstacles. Now that the higher court sent the case back for a new trial, skepticism had been revived. "Just when a new information will be filed by the prosecuting attorney is not known," the *Star* reported. "It is already predicted there will be more delays."

Six weeks into his apprenticeship, Hemingway achieved a breakthrough in his writing. He fashioned a feature story, a full column long in the big Sunday paper, which devoured all the human interest tales the staff could churn out. The story was surrounded by department store ads for furs, Goldberg the tailor, beauty parlors, and Rain Water Shampoo, which had the quality of removing "superfluous hair." The story didn't cost Hemingway much in the way of shoe leather, given that his profile subject was a clerk at the *Star*, but it allowed him to get in the ring with one of his favorite boyhood interests: boxing. The subject's name was Leo Kobreen. He'd earned a reputation as a scrappy newsboy fighter. Of tiny stature, he qualified as a bantamweight when he graduated from street corners to the ring. An illustration, based on a photograph, shows him in a cardigan sweater with collar and a contrasting placket, baggy pants, and ankle boots. He wears a tie, holds his hands behind his back, and looks at what must have been the camera with a serious, closemouthed expression. He's standing next to an office desk, whose top comes nearly to his chest; he's

An illustration of Leo Kobreen accompanied Hemingway's profile of the diminutive boxer. *Kansas City Star*

"inches short of five feet," Hemingway wrote, and because he had the face of a well-known Russian recently in the news and was indeed an immigrant from Kiev, he was handed the nickname Kerensky. (Alexander Kerensky, a principal of the Russian Revolution, had just a few weeks before this story appeared been ousted by Vladimir Lenin and forced into exile.)

Hemingway's story about Leo Kobreen* carries evidence of the writer's skills as a close observer. Aside from the use of typical interview quotes, it also includes moments of narrative dialogue, a hallmark of Hemingway's later fiction. As with several of the most accomplished *Star* narratives attributed to Hemingway, readers and scholars must wrestle with a fundamental question of authorship. How much of these stories came out of Hemingway's typing mill fully formed, and how much credit goes to Pete Wellington, his principal editor, or other line editors manhandling his copy? Still,

---

*Reproduced in full in the appendix.

all of that editorial activity contributed to Hemingway's education, and the evidence is on the page. Even in this piece of his journalistic juvenilia—he later expressed horror that anyone would read the early stuff—a certain fundamental voice of the mature Hemingway whispers: "Somehow, although he is the smallest office boy around the place, none of the other lads pick on him. Scuffling and fighting almost has ceased since Kerensky came to work. That's only one of the nicknames of Leo Kobreen, and was assigned to him because of a considerable facial resemblance to the perpetually fleeing Russian statesman, and, too, because both wore quite formal standing collars." Kobreen hated the smoke that typically surrounded the boxing ring. "But of course," he told Hemingway, ". . . if I knew some of the clubs downtown had a smoker on and they offered me $2, of course I'd get in and fight."

At the end of the story, Hemingway includes an awareness of the Russian Civil War that followed the revolution that fall. Anti-Semitism abounded among those who opposed the Bolsheviks. It's only a brief subtheme, but it gives depth to the boxer profile, the sort of embedded sense of history that Hemingway would ever employ:

After hard days in old Russia, the life is full of joy for Leo, and who can say that he is not making the most of his opportunities? When he talks of the past it is of a pogram [sic]. That Christmas season the workmen in a sugar refinery near Kiev made a cross of ice and set it up on the frozen river. It fell over and they blamed the Jews. Then the workmen rioted, breaking into stores and smashing windows. Leo and his family hid on the roof for three days, and his sister fell ill of pneumonia. One studies to change the subject and asks:

"Leo, do they ever match you with a bigger boy?"

"Oh no," he says, "the crowd wouldn't stand for that. But sometimes I catch one on the street."

Hemingway had written a boxing story in high school. He staged boxing matches in the drawing room of the family home in Oak Park. In coming years boxers would populate his writing off and on. So Leo Kobreen was one in a line that extends from Robert Cohn, the college boxing champ in *The Sun Also Rises*, to the ravaged fighter Ad Francis in "The Battler," to the real-life fighter Larry Gains, whom Hemingway sketched in his Paris memoir. Each of Hemingway's boxing pieces tries to measure the making of winners and losers, and his successive narrators gather a certain wisdom in quite different stylistic ways. "Kerensky, the Fighting Flea" was only a beginning. Regardless of its literary value, it helps point out that Hemingway already was becoming familiar with the battling streets of Kansas City.

Crime items routinely documented robberies, beatings, and knifings on North End streets, and Hemingway gathered much of the bloody action at the hospital or the police station on Nineteenth Street. But another sort of battle was arising out of the streetscape where grassroots power and money collided. It was a struggle for political domination. Hemingway caught wind of it in the W. C. Bowman story, but bigger names gained more attention in the newsroom.

Thomas J. Pendergast, for example, was the youngest brother of Jim Pendergast, the West Bottoms saloon keeper and power broker who had built a ward-boss network of influence beginning in the 1890s. After Jim Pendergast died in 1911, Tom, who'd earlier served as the city's superintendent of streets, was elected to his brother's former seat on the city council. By 1916 the Pendergast machine had solidly coalesced around Tom. He'd left the council the year before but wielded considerable influence among Jackson County Democrats. He gathered power by looking out for the working-class poor in the First Ward, helping to supply coal and food to the needy. At a Pendergast Christmas party in 1917, during Hemingway's winter in Kansas City, he fed more than twenty-five hundred people. He was boss of the "goats" faction of the party, which shared power with Joe Shannon's "rabbits" and developed an uneasy alliance with an upstart group led by Miles Bulger of the Second Ward. Pendergast's economic interests included liquor, cement, and some of those boardinghouses of questionable character that were attracting increasing attention in the city's crackdown on vice. As the new year neared, Pendergast was working toward a political takeover of the city and thinking about a slate of candidates for elections in March and November.

The *Star* reported on the power plays behind the scenes involving jobs at city hall, the police department, county road crews, and more. Hemingway would've learned how power and wealth intertwined in Kansas City. Around his uncle's dinner table he'd hear of W. T. Kemper, the wealthy banker who'd struck it rich in railroads and oil and, in the newspaper's estimation, was a solid ally of Pendergast. "When the gong sounds for the mayor's race," the newspaper reported one December day, "Pendergast and W.T. Kemper will be found backing the same candidate, all reports to a possible split between the two men to the contrary. Pendergast makes no secret of the fact that he is 'for anything Mr. Kemper wants.'"

Another lesson in power unfolded over one of Pendergast's holdings, the Jefferson Hotel at 601 Wyandotte Street. Politicos gathered there frequently, and a cabaret operated in the basement. But it had a reputation for assignations and abundant drink, and it invited suggestions that police and the North Side court judge looked the other way. In the civic crackdown on vice, the Jefferson, "the most notorious of vice centers," became a prominent target.

After the secretary of war threatened to close off the city to soldiers, Mayor Edwards went after the place and wanted to make it an example for others who weren't paying attention to the booze crisis. "Close the Jefferson Hotel," Edwards announced at one meeting. "That will throw the fear of God in the hearts of the little fellows who are operating." But of course it wasn't that easy. Pendergast had friends in high places, and one police commissioner, John R. Ranson, did his bidding: in that meeting of city officials he refused to vote to shut the Jefferson down. It's not difficult to imagine Hemingway reporting in the midst of this kind of civic controversy. As he told his sister, "I can tell mayors to go to Hell and slap police commissioners on the Back!"

———

In early December, Hemingway moved again. He joined Carl Edgar in a dormered upstairs room of a wood-frame house at 3516 Agnes Avenue. It was "a nice big room with easy chairs and a table and dresser and a sleeping porch with two big double beds for $2.50 apiece per week." One of Edgar's coworkers at the California Fuel Oil Co. also lived in the house. Hemingway could use the electric streetcar line on Prospect, four blocks away, to get downtown and back. But more important, the move gave Hemingway even more physical distance from his uncle than Mrs. Haynes's boardinghouse afforded. He was also out from under the obligation of Mrs. Haynes's dinner call, which interrupted work every night, he complained. It gave him greater freedom to work at will and to "jazz forth" with Carl Edgar and other friends.

There were Saturday night poker games with Todd Ormiston. There were bull sessions at Pecoraro's Italian joint at Fifth and Walnut Streets in the North End, where Hemingway sat quietly absorbing the journalistic wisdom of his elders as they downed spaghetti and *polpette*. Pecoraro's, a second-floor place above a saloon near police headquarters, was most likely the watering hole where Hemingway learned to "distinguish chianti, catawba, malvasia, Dago Red, claret and several others sans the use of the eyes," as he boasted to his sister.

December brought a cold wave and brutal winds, which Hemingway endured with a big red sweater under his mackinaw. That helped him get through a couple weeks of below-zero temperatures. He also got the help of an overcoat supplied by the Missouri Guard. "They are regulation like the uniform and warm as the dickens," he told his parents. His father had sent him some army shoes, and a Michigan friend, Marge Bump, had knitted him a "peach of a sweater," an army-style slip-on. Those items helped him endure guard drills in the cold, and he was grateful for the overcoat because it would come in handy if his new sleeping porch got much colder.

Among Hemingway's occasional reporting responsibilities was a sweep through the Union Station train terminal. That was one leg of the "short-stop" run, which included Police Station No. 4 and General Hospital. You never knew who'd be passing through or what human drama the cops, porters, and coffee slingers would be talking about. One Saturday night, a train hauling forty-five black soldiers convicted of charges stemming from a mutinous race riot in Houston passed through Kansas City on the way to the federal penitentiary in Leavenworth. "There were three special cars of them and three guards armed with rifles at each end of each car," he wrote. Hemingway was a young man of his era, and evidence of social consciousness is fleeting, though not entirely missing. His underdeveloped attitudes toward race can be ascertained by the language he employed when writing about African Americans in the *Star* of those days and in his fiction and letters of subsequent years. Neither the *Star* nor Hemingway refrained from using the *n*-word, the slur that must have felt all too comfortable coming off his tongue. Though the *Star* spoke more directly to the city's white population, it did manage to find brief corners to take paternalistic note of racial developments, including a public forum where the topic would be "the uplift of the negro race."

The evolving sound of jazz could be heard across Kansas City in 1917. The Shubert Theater advertised a jazz orchestra "with banjos, saxophones and marimbaphone" that would keep listeners "swaying in your seat to the irresistible rhythm." The relatively new art form, which had emanated out of New Orleans, already permeated the language. In one letter home, Hemingway went full out: "J-Z-Z-Z-Z-Z-Z-Z-z-z-z-z-z-z-z." The music was somewhat feared by the straight and narrow, and that fall it was banned from military dances in New York. Nevertheless jazz offered creative temptations to the adventurous and a kind of salve for the anxieties brought by war and other uncertainties. One *Star* writer, very likely Russel Crouse, the future playwright who once admitted to being a regular at Kansas City's burlesque houses, dove deep into the jazz-tinged cabaret life to take a certain pulse: "The major and minor tragedies of life and the times may crash around unhappy heads and bow them low, but the ragtime entertainers of the night life cafes continue on their hilarious way, unaffected and unchanged by the stress of these parlous times." The story was intended to show that despite a recent downturn in the theater world the basement grills operating as cabarets still had some life in them, or at least were "showing a final rally before they are borne down and crushed by the sterner things that are at hand."

The headline writer went straight for the offbeat—WHERE THE "NUT STUFF" PAYS—taking a cue from the reporter's description of the vaudeville-inspired character singer, also known as the "nut singer." The feature included long quotes from such a performer, revealing the odd workings of the entertainment business:

> "No wonder we're nutty," explains one frank young man whose nightly antics are the delight of the Twelfth Street pleasure workers. "In the first place we had to be born that way to be entertainers. No sane man or woman would or could hold down a job like mine. We never get to talk to anybody. When we get through work everybody is asleep except the policemen and a cop's no company for anybody

An illustration accompanied a story about cabaret singers, WHERE THE "NUT STUFF" PAYS. *Kansas City Star*

not even a cabaret singer and comedian. Even actors hit the
hay hours before we wash up and start home. But at that,
when we get out of the shop no one takes us seriously. You
tell them, brother, the entertainer is nothing but a blue note
among mankind and you can't judge him too rough—the
poor nut."

The story explained that there were four kinds of cabaret singers: ragtime, character, ballads, and semiclassical. "The revue style
of entertainment that is in vogue in New York finds an echo in
Kansas City and one café has a chorus of six girls who support
the principals." Cabaret operators were always interested in trying
new things, and one had announced he would take a gamble on
reviving interest in light opera—*Pinafore, The Mikado, The Bohe-
mian Girl.* Many of the singers, who often came from traveling
musical comedies, bounced from club to club, and the whole
cabaret operation "has no assured future," the writer noted, as
Prohibition loomed.

Aside from introducing Hemingway to the precarious netherworld of entertainment, to the "smash of the barbaric jazz"—he'd
already been exposed at home to the higher culture of opera—
his colleague's story gave him an extended example of a writer
capturing a vernacular voice of the day. It was another lesson in
narrative dialogue:

"Sure, I know it looks like a swell job. Nothin' to do but sing
and make a nut out of yourself. It looks like a cinch, but we
got hardships same as anyone else. Didn't we have a shirt
salesman here the other night that was tippin' us right and left
for singin' 'I Don't Want to Get Well?' Sure, the money was
comin' in, brother, but how would you like to keep singin'
that one song or another one song—time after time the most

part of the evenin'? It was killin' us with the rest of the house, but what could we do?"

Hemingway was no stranger to Kansas City's nightlife. "I do not doubt that he visited whatever dives he could find," Carl Edgar recalled years later. "I should say however as an observer rather than a patron." Other friends provide details of more active experiences sampling the liquid haunts of Twelfth Street. And the memory of Kansas City's cabarets would have lingered in Hemingway's mind. Only a few years later he would be hearing the "barbaric jazz" and the nutty singers in the night scenes of Paris.

———————————

Hemingway apologized to his parents that work kept him so occupied that he didn't have time to write. "Just the regular line of stuff, but plenty of it," he said. He expected even to work on Christmas Day. Speaking of which, he was sorry that his package of Christmas gifts would be late, because his next paycheck wasn't due until the following week. But the never-ending rhythm of the city demanded Hemingway's presence and filled his days. There were holdup gangs, a "Bandit Queen," and police nailing street criminals. There were streetcar accidents, including a fatality when a young Iowa soldier on furlough lost a hand, then his life, after falling off a car. There were coal shortages. And there were troubles brewing in the city's hospitals, the beat that would consume much of Hemingway's time in the winter months.

8

THE AMBULANCE RUN

*I have had At least ½ column every day for the last week in my end.
We have got them on the run I think.*
—HEMINGWAY TO HIS FAMILY

The war effort was wreaking havoc on Kansas City's General Hospital. Staffers were commissioned into service. The government was wresting nurses away with attractive pay and benefits. The ambulance surgeons Hemingway had gotten to know in the first weeks of his apprenticeship were leaving to report for duty at Fort Riley. Dr. Ben A. Salzberg. Dr. Harry Dugay. Dr. Forrest F. Foster. Dr. F. E. Dargatz. All were heading out by mid-December. "The General Hospital faces a grave crippling of its staff due to present war conditions," said Dr. Elliott Washburn, its business manager. Washburn feared that most of the nurses in training would spring for the government's bigger paychecks, fifty dollars a month and expenses as opposed to the ten dollars a month and board they got from the training school. The hospital would have to attract more than twenty young women for its training program in the coming weeks.

Hemingway had already earned a reputation in the newsroom for disappearing on ambulance runs with Salzberg and the others. He later captured the woozy feel of it in an unpublished sketch, describing the motion of a vehicle as it sped away from the hospital. The fragment marks the first appearance of a Doc Fisher, one of two surgeons aboard. Years later, Hemingway would call on a Doc Fischer for a role as a central character in a fully formed short story, "God Rest You Merry, Gentleman," whose setting was also the Kansas City General Hospital. This surgeon was "thin, sand-blond, with a thin mouth," a description that echoes quite closely Hemingway's earlier sketch about Doc Kling, the drug addict. They also both had "gambler's hands."

The hospital beat became Hemingway's main midwinter event. The medical community was embroiled in intertwining crises, which provided Hemingway with material for more than two months. The Apperson ambulances, for example, were capable of impressive speed, although, as Hemingway experienced, they were not always reliably in service. And soon the staffing shortages, compounded by equipment breakdowns, began to affect the public's health. Hemingway one day reported the regretful story of a man trapped and seriously injured in an apparel store's elevator shaft. An ambulance was called but broke down on its way. Two of the city's three ambulances were already in a garage following accidents, and it took two hours before a private ambulance could arrive and haul the man to the hospital.

To make matters worse, the city had been experiencing an outbreak of smallpox. So many cases had been reported—247 people under quarantine on one December night—that the city health board planned to reopen a closed building to operate an isolation hospital. Vaccinations of school children became an urgent priority. News stories reported the daily developments. Hemingway began one story with a narrative scene:

> The raggedy man pushed his way through a crowd of school children waiting to be vaccinated at the Emergency Hospital this morning. Entering the elevator he asked for Dr. Fred W. Coon, and was taken to his office.
>
> "Doctor, I believe I've got smallpox," he said.
>
> "I know it," said Doctor Coon, rising and hurrying out.
>
> The raggedy man leaned back in his chair, braced his feet on a desk and for two hours was the sole occupant of the office. The working force moved to the next floor and a hasty search for fumigating sprayers was started.
>
> There was no place to send the patient. The contagion wing at the General hospital is crowded with smallpox patients.

For Christmas 1917, Hemingway's mother sent him a book, *An Explorer's Adventures in Tibet*, by A. Henry Savage Landor. It was the kind of book that would feed Hemingway's appetite for fearlessly taking on the world and all its dangers. (And it was good enough to last, given that it remained in Hemingway's library for the rest of his life.) Hemingway might have had time to read some of it during that day's holiday shift. He worked, but it was relatively quiet in the newsroom, which collectively gathered tidbits from charity Christmas meals and a murder case the night before.

With the new year Kansas City's hospital problems worsened and kept Hemingway busy. City health officials were dropping the ball. "Kansas City," one of Hemingway's stories began, "is being exposed every day to smallpox because of a lack of facilities for caring for patients, and officials responsible continue to disclaim responsibility." A woman with the disease was allowed to stay for three days at St. Anthony's Home for Infants, despite the fact that her case had been reported to Dr. W. H. Coon, the city health director. City councilmen were told on a Monday night that an ill man was in a hotel, not named by the paper, for two days, unable to get admitted to the city hospital. And just that morning, a woman called the mayor's office to complain that the health officials had yet to respond to her report of a smallpox case in her rooming house two days earlier. At least half a dozen such cases had been reported, but Coon replied that his hospital beds were filled and he could get no money to expand. That morning he emphasized to Hemingway that he'd been trying. "Every time the question has been raised," Coon said, "I have been told there was no money available."

The city comptroller, Eugene Blake, acknowledged a funding shortage but pointed the finger at Coon. "I was present," Blake said, "when Mayor Edwards told Doctor Coon and the health board, if it appeared to be necessary, to go ahead and rent and equip quarters for smallpox patients. That was at least three weeks ago and if no provision has been made since it is not the fault of the administration." Blake told Hemingway that in an emergency the city could find the funds. The newspaper clearly was aiming its sights at Coon, and Hemingway was much in the thick of it.

As if smallpox weren't enough, Hemingway called in a report of an outbreak of spinal meningitis at the James Elementary School, on the city's northeast side. Two sisters had been admitted to the isolation ward at General Hospital and their mother died, Hemingway reported. Dr. Coon ordered every student at the school under observation. Soon that outbreak snowballed into another crisis. A man named Erwin Gast became the second fatal victim in late January. General Hospital counted at least eight active cases and was on the verge of declaring an epidemic. The *Star*, probably Hemingway, asserted that "new and more stringent methods must be adopted by the health department to check this disease as well as smallpox."

The health board was under siege, and Hemingway, the young and eager reporter, was among those leading the charge. "We are making a big fight on the Hospital and Health board," he wrote to his mother. "The politicians on the Board have grafted $27,000 since the first of the year. . . . I cover all the Hospital and investigation end of the hospital graft." He put in lots of extra hours and worked hard to "get and verify dangerous facts and prove them beyond the shadow of a libel suit." Julian Capers, a United Press reporter who got to know Hemingway at the time, recounted later that Hemingway's assignment led to a series of stories meant to remove "an arrogant and inefficient superintendent."

One legendary story about Hemingway and the smallpox beat involved an episode of alleged heroism. A man with smallpox had collapsed at Union Station. An ambulance was taking far too long to collect him, and Hemingway purportedly picked the man up, carried him to a cab, and accompanied him to General Hospital. That's the gist of Ted Brumback's account, which he delivered in his remembrance for the *Star* in 1936. Years later, Hemingway's fourth wife, Mary Welsh Hemingway, told much the same story, which she said her husband recounted for her more than once. Trouble is, it doesn't exactly square with the news story—unfortunately, a rather convoluted one—that Hemingway filed one Monday in February:

While the chauffeur and male nurse on the city ambulance devoted to the carrying of smallpox cases drove from the General Hospital to the municipal garage on the North Side today to have engine trouble "fixed" a man, his face and hands covered with smallpox pustules, lay in one of the entrances to the Union Station. One hour and fifteen minutes after having been given the call the chauffeur and nurse reported at the hospital with the man, G.T. Brewer, 926 West Forty-second Street. The ambulance had been repaired.

The story went on to describe a series of mechanical and communications breakdowns.

One could conclude that, if you believe the legend, Hemingway or his editors left his own heroism out of the story. But if the nurse and the chauffeur transported the sick man to the hospital, as the story reported, what was Hemingway's role? Was this a Hemingway invention, told so convincingly that Brumback and Mary Hemingway couldn't help but believe it and repeat it decades later? Was it another epic expression of self-important exaggeration that the young man would engage in for the rest of his life?

At the end of the story, Hemingway quoted a doctor who "criticized the police for failure to remove Brewer to an isolated place instead of leaving him 'where scores of travelers came in contact and were exposed to smallpox.'" Again, Hemingway's reporting appears to undermine the legend.

A housecleaning began at the hospital in late January. The business manager, Dr. E. W. Washburn, was dismissed, though he stayed on in the health department to run the milk inspection program. The health board, largely controlled by Republicans rather than Pendergast's Democrats, was suspicious. The board president wanted an inventory of hospital supplies, because "things have been leaving the hospital and they do not know where they have gone." Also ousted was Dr. E. H. Trowbridge, who had organized school inspections and served in various capacities with the department. The board also began to address the capacity shortage, adding fifty beds to the smallpox isolation ward that had been installed at the tuberculosis hospital in the Leeds district, in the river bottoms east of downtown. The board intended to do something about the ambulance situation as well, trying to limit breakdowns by enforcing a thirty-mile-an-hour speed limit on drivers and firing one chauffeur who'd been hired at an excessive wage. The board expanded emergency service to twenty-four hours a day and added two telephone trunk lines at General Hospital to ensure a better response to the increasing reports of disease.

Hemingway was particularly proud of the effect his reporting had on the hospital squabbles. According to one account, the hospital director once threw him out, and one friend suggested fisticuffs ensued. As for the value of Hemingway's daily experience of chasing ambulances and exploring the human drama of Kansas City, one of his most accomplished stories came off the hospital beat. Headlined AT THE END OF THE AMBULANCE RUN,* the story was built as a composition of narrative episodes. The assemblage of vignettes led Matthew Bruccoli and other literary scholars to conclude logically that it presaged Hemingway's vignette experiments in Paris just a few years later. This is the opening section:

> The night ambulance attendants shuffled down the long, dark corridors at the General Hospital with an inert burden on the stretcher. They turned in at the receiving ward and lifted

---

*Reproduced in full in the appendix.

the unconscious man to the operating table. His hands were calloused and he was unkempt and ragged, a victim of a street brawl near the city market. No one knew who he was, but a receipt, bearing the name of George Anderson, for $10 paid on a home out in a little Nebraska town served to identify him.

The surgeon opened the swollen eyelids. The eyes were turned to the left. "A fracture on the left side of the skull," he said to the attendants who stood about the table. "Well, George, you're not going to finish paying for that home of yours."

"George" merely lifted a hand as though groping for something. Attendants hurriedly caught hold of him to keep him from rolling from the table. But he scratched his face in a tired, resigned way that seemed almost ridiculous, and placed his hand again at his side. Four hours later he died.

It was merely one of the many cases that come to the city dispensary from night to night—and from day to day for that matter; but the night shift, perhaps, has a wider range of the life and death tragedy—and even comedy, of the city. When "George" comes in on the soiled, bloody stretcher and the rags are stripped off and his naked, broken body lies on the white table in the glare of the surgeon's light, and he dangles on a little thread of life, while the physicians struggle grimly, it is all in the night's work, whether the thread snaps or whether it holds so that George can fight on and work and play.

There is no evidence to determine how long Hemingway worked on this story, though clearly he had gathered material on more than one occasion. He and his editors must have taken extra time to order up illustrations from the newsroom's art department and to polish the prose. Surely an erudite editor, working with Hemingway on an episode about a wounded printer, suggested the allusion of "a French artist who vowed to commit suicide if he lost his right hand in battle" to the patient's struggle "alone in the darkness."

Still, AT THE END OF THE AMBULANCE RUN gives a vivid example of Hemingway using detail to great effect. Moreover, it reflects Hemingway's sense of Kansas City as a tableaux of street fights,

A *Star* sketch artist put together a collage to accompany Hemingway's ambulance-run feature. *Kansas City Star*

shootings, and violent death. Everyone dies, but death by violence makes for stories. In his scene-setting, Hemingway enters the teeming world right away. The observation that as doctors worked on him, the man lifted his hand and "scratched his face in a tired, resigned way that seemed almost ridiculous" feels rather harsh or arrogant or even callously juvenile. Yet the young Hemingway was learning from the operations of the night shift, which "has a wider range of the life and death and tragedy—and even comedy, of the city."

Bruccoli acknowledged a clear connection between these articles and *In Our Time*, as well as the later short story "God Rest You Merry, Gentlemen" (1933). And, Bruccoli added, the "Negro who refuses to identify his assailant anticipates Cayetano of 'The Gambler, the Nun, and the Radio' (1933). In addition to the violent material, other characteristics of Hemingway's later work are to be seen in these vignettes: the unsentimental tone, the presentation of character through speech, and the use of detail."

Hemingway, the writer in training, was developing the eye and the patience to record the smallest of moments to punctuate his tale and to emphasize the fragility of the thread of life—the "broken body" in the "glare of the surgeon's light"; a red handkerchief hanging from an alleged robber's neck.

In a stylistic bit of illuminated symmetry, the story begins with the surgeon's glaring light and ends with an ambulance leaving the hospital, racing down the Cherry Street hills, "the headlights boring a yellow funnel into the darkness." The newly developed apostle of the violent had here announced that he, too, "was boring a yellow funnel" into the dangerous matters of the world.

9

CRIME AND PUNISHMENT

And the old icy wind blows straight down from Athabasca
down the Mo. River valley and penetrate to the bones
of the frigid Steinway. In other words she are cold.
—HEMINGWAY TO HIS FAMILY

By 8:30 on a Friday night, the temperature plunged to twenty below zero at Camp Funston, the army's training facility on the Kansas prairie at Fort Riley, a few hours west of Kansas City. Capt. Lewis J. Whisler had spent a few minutes pacing furtively in a room at the YWCA Hostess House, and then walked into the night, sure of what he had to do. He knocked on the door of the army bank. It had closed for the day, but five men were still there. Once inside, Whisler raised a handgun and ordered, "Hands up!" He pulled pieces of rope from his overcoat pocket, tossed them toward Kearney Wornall, a bank cashier, and told him to tie up the others' hands and feet. Whisler tied Wornall with one hand, his revolver in the other, and gagged them all. From within his overcoat he pulled out an ax. He began wielding it, butchering the five men one after the other, attacking their heads and faces with the butt and the blade. Whisler looted the safe but overlooked a drawer full of gold and currency. He returned to his room in the barracks of the Second Battalion, 364th Infantry. At 9:00 PM, he reported to regimental school for an hour. Police later speculated that sometime thereafter he shipped the loot, $65,000 or more, somewhere by mail, although other theories had not yet been ruled out: one, that he hid the stash, and two, that he'd had an accomplice. The next afternoon Whisler learned that one of the victims of the attack had survived—it was Wornall, the last man Whisler hastily assaulted—and thus could identify him as the slayer. At 2:00 PM he shot himself (twice) with a rifle. Army officials denied the intimation that he had been granted an unwritten law of the service, which, in order to maintain "the honor of the army," gives a grievously errant officer the chance to commit suicide. Evidence emerged that Whisler, recently divorced, desperate for money, and in love with a seventeen-year-old girl, had been obsessed with suicide and had devised this very scheme leading to that fate.

Hemingway did not cover this sensational crime, but he, and everyone else in the newsroom and the reading public, was riveted by details of the story as they emerged over several days. A large engraving in the paper showed the bloody crime scene after the victims' bodies had been removed. A few days later, the *Star* provided another lesson for the young reporter in how violence shaped the stuff of literature. One of the paper's literary staffers explored how the Funston ax murders seemed straight out of Dostoyevsky. "A man is born," the piece begins. "For thirty-seven years he does nothing to make him conspicuous above or below his fellows. Then he kills, brutally, without provocation, almost without attempt at concealment, with a motive and in a manner which shut the door of escape. Why? Probably Capt. Lewis Whisler never heard of Dostoievsky; but the man who has been called the greatest of Russian writers knew Whisler—knew him as none knew him who called him by name; knew the murky, melancholic, introspective mental path he trod to the end."

The literary analysis served as one more piece of the newsroom's college syllabus for a budding writer such as Hemingway. The anonymous writer had a compelling sense of drama and clearly had a handle on the depths of the Russian's tale:

> "Long ago his present anguish had its beginnings; it had waxed and gathered strength, it had matured and concentrated until it had taken the form of a fearful, frenzied, fantastic question which tortured his heart and his mind, clamoring instantly for an answer."

Dostoievsky wrote that about Raskolnikov in *Crime and Punishment*. It might have been written about Whisler.

The comparison continued in several more passages:

Raskolnikov borrowed an ax to kill a pawnbroker. He, too, made a previous call on his victim, to "rehearse" the crime. When the day came—it was almost the same hour—he, too, gained entrance on a plea of urgent business. He, too, wore no disguise. He, too, had no reason to expect to find any other person there, but he did.

The first blow Whisler struck with the ax in the army bank at Camp Funston was not a hard blow. It did not stun his victim. The first blow Raskolnikov struck with the ax was not a hard blow.

"His hands were fearfully weak . . . but as soon as he had brought the ax down his strength returned. . . . He was in full possession of his faculties."

Then a man tried to gain admittance to the pawnbroker's room. While Whisler was robbing the bank a man tried to gain admittance.

The Russian hid his loot in the wall of his room. So did Whisler.

Raskolnikov, too, would have committed suicide, but for the merest chance.

The Whisler-Raskolnikov essay went on for twenty-eight more paragraphs, mining the parallels between the real-life character and the fictional one, connections that "extended deep into the temperaments and impulses of the men." But where there were differences between the invented and real individuals, "it was because the fiction character, in the minutest workings of his brain, was presented by a master analyst, whereas there was none to know, save from the events, how the brain of the army captain functioned."

Not long after the ax murder story, Hemingway became an avowed admirer of the Russian writers. He read Dostoyevsky during his Paris education, which began four years after his Kansas City education, and though he felt that the Russian writer was inadequate—"How can a man write so badly, so unbelievably badly, and make you feel so deeply?"—he admired and respected his place in the pantheon. Hemingway's friend Ted Brumback once told him that even without a college degree, he'd do fine as a writer. All he had to do was read a psychology textbook. And here was a *Star* writer planting that seed as well, exploring the psychology of two men, one tragically real, one masterfully fictional. Hemingway's colleague, indeed, imbued Dostoyevsky with the power of "a master analyst." Fiction writers can shape the consciousnesses of their characters in ways that journalists writing about real life often don't—another lesson Hemingway was learning and one that finally sank in when he came under Gertrude Stein's tutelage four years later. As Charles Fenton put it, "Miss Stein had been emphatic in her insistence that a writer must create rather than merely report."

Another running story Hemingway kept up with was the murder trial of Mary A. Kreiser. She was accused of killing her husband, Edward, an organist of the Independence Boulevard Christian Church. In mid-January, the judge granted a fourth continuance, this time because a key witness was serving in the army in France. The witness worked in a hardware store and, on the night before the homicide, sold a woman alleged to be Kreiser a .32-caliber revolver. On hearing the judge's ruling, Kreiser burst out crying. The strain of prosecution had impeded her life for the last year. Now she'd have to wait till May, or even until the war was over. Her lawyer was prepared to argue an insanity defense. Her husband had freely admitted he'd had immoral relations with his music pupils and other women and taunted his wife with the news. Given the story's proximity to the Whisler coverage on a cold day in January, the hot human drama was ripe stuff for a writer in the making. Indeed, Hemingway would eventually produce a vivid short story about a woman who shoots her husband, "The Short Happy Life of Francis Macomber."

The staffers on the exchange desk one day gave Hemingway another college-curriculum-level opportunity, this time to ponder the influence of Henry James. The American author had died the previous year, and the op-ed page excerpted one of his last articles, which had appeared in *Harper's* magazine. Hemingway would have recognized the mark of a great writer, though James's prose flowed with the kind of opulent style he would eventually reject and actively overturn as he crafted the modernist foundation of American literature:

It was in the first place, after the strangest fashion, a sense of the extraordinary way in which the most benign conditions of light and air, of sky and sea, the most beautiful English summer conceivable, mixed themselves with all the violence of action and passion, the other so hideous and piteous, so heroic and tragic facts, and flouted them as with the example of something far superior. Never were desperate doings so blandly lighted up as by the two unforgettable months that I was to spend so much of in looking over from the old rampart of a little high-perched Sussex town at the bright blue streak of the Channel, within a mile or two of us at its nearest point, the point to which it had receded after washing our rock base in its earlier ages; and staring at the bright mystery beyond the rim of the furthest opaline reach. Just on the other side of that finest of horizon lines history was raging at a pitch new under the sun; thinly masked by that shameless smile the Belgian horror grew; the curve of the globe toward these things was of the scantest, and yet the hither spaces of the purest, the interval representing only charm and calm and east. . . . Just over that line were unutterable things, massacre and ravage and anguish, all but irresistible assault and cruelty, bewilderment and heroism all but overwhelmed; from the sense of which one had but to turn one's head to take in something unspeakable different and that yet produced, as by some extraordinary paradox, a pang almost as sharp.

Today's reader might wish James had gotten to his point more quickly and more clearly. Hemingway might have appreciated the tone poem as it bloomed, but he also could have reacted to it as something like the last gasp of Victorian literature. Nevertheless there was something memorable in it: the "unutterable things, massacre and ravage and anguish . . . and heroism all but overwhelmed." Ten years later Hemingway would unspool a related idea about language and anxiety in his novel of the same war on which James was meditating. "There were many words that you could not stand to hear," Hemingway would write in *A Farewell to Arms*, "and finally only the names of places had dignity. . . . Abstract words such as glory, honor, courage, or hallow were obscene beside the concrete names of villages, the numbers of roads, the names of rivers, the numbers of regiments and the dates." Clear and direct and provocative.

For now, though, the war was a shifting idea in Hemingway's head. He knew he would somehow become involved, would join up with the Canadians, the marines, whoever would have him. He had told his parents in November that he'd work until spring. He couldn't imagine staying out of the war beyond that. And in early January, he reported that he and two friends, probably Ted Brumback and Charles Hopkins, would head to Michigan on May 1, then "enlist together in the Marines in the fall unless I can get into aviation when I am 19 and get a commission." (Burris Jenkins had written affectionately about aviators, perhaps impressing the idea upon Hemingway.) The truth is, Hemingway couldn't pass the required physicals. The strapping boy had a weak eye and flat feet. Soon, however, another opportunity would emerge to ensure Hemingway's involvement in the war.

The phone rang at Hemingway's house. His boss was on the other end of the line. Head down to a fire, he said, at Eighteenth and Holmes, just a few blocks from the *Star*'s building. "Well I went and got the yarn and telephoned for a photographer and got soaked all through my shoes in the icy water," Hemingway wrote to his family. The fire had broken out at three in the morning amid a pile of greasy rags. By the time Hemingway arrived on the scene, three businesses in the Holtman Building had been destroyed: the Holtman Heating Co., the Automatic Machine Co., and the Western Paper Box Co. Investigators estimated damages at $187,000, half of which was covered by insurance, Hemingway reported. The blaze even spread to nearby buildings, though the brief story did not elaborate. Hemingway sloshed in his wet shoes four blocks to the office, where he had stashed some wool socks in his locker. His grandmother had sent him a new pair, and he was grateful for the gesture, which allowed him to change into "the warm wool jazzy ones" and become "ready to step forth among them."

In the midst of the newspaper's manpower shortage caused by the war, Hemingway worked as many extra hours as he could. He was energized by the action and felt downright important to the campaign to improve the hospital and health board. His sense of Kansas City was heightened by newsroom chatter, by after-hours bull sessions, and by whatever he picked up on the streets. "There is going to be lots doing soon when the spring campaign for the city election starts," he told his parents. "This is as dirty a political town as the old smoke ville on the lake Mich."

An assignment sheet from January 3, 1918, shows an editor had penciled in Hemingway for several stories. *Reproduced in* Ernest Hemingway, Cub Reporter, *edited by Matthew J. Bruccoli*

Not everything Hemingway covered had the urgent glamour of graft and blood. And not everything he experienced had the literary gravity of the Camp Funston ax murders. In early February he spent a few days writing routine features from a farm implement exposition at Union Station. A tractor show was filled with funny and weird machines, about 150 different ones. "I thought I was having a night mare," he told his grandmother. "A lot of them look unreal, like great big autos with wheels 15 feet high." After several days of news and notes from this prominent annual affair, including one story that speculated on the need for women to drive tractors as their farming men went to war, a gala party marked the end with style. The celebration was "a smoker de luxe." Plans were announced for the tractor show of 1919. Vaudeville entertainers enlivened the evening along with "classy acts": "two women singers, who went strong; a burlesque dancer, a male soloist, magician, contortionist, Chief Silvertongue [sic], the Indian tenor; a group of negro song and dance artists, and as the announcer stated, 'one special act to remind the boys of home,' which was a sparring match between a stockily built young woman and dodging bear."

Hemingway occasionally reviewed theatrical events and vaudeville shows, and he took in the movies and other entertainment on Twelfth Street and elsewhere around town. He boasted to his sister that he had crossed paths with a movie star, and indeed was smitten. It's quite possible that Mae Marsh, star of the recent hits *Polly of the Circus*, *The Cinderella Man*, and *Fields of Honor*, alighted from a train at Union Station and overnighted at the Muehlebach Hotel. The "girl of a thousand faces" was on her way to the East Coast to make another movie. "I have met the fair one and have fell hard," he said. Hemingway was hungry for love and imagined Mae Marsh as "the future Mrs. Hemingstein." Hemingway seemed to be in competition with Wilson "Lackpants" Hicks, the *Star*'s movie editor, but "she loves me a whole lot better or else she is a darn liar." According to

Hemingway, Marsh promised to wait for him if he went off to war. Hicks apparently did not write about the local appearance of the beautiful young actress. But to hear Hemingway swoon in a letter to his sister, the episode seems like a peak personal experience: "Oh Boy. Oh Man. Oh Hemingstein. I could rave on for hours." Hemingway urged his sister to see Marsh's movies and to imagine her brother receiving the actress's letters and even a signed picture.

Just a few months later, as Hemingway prepared to ship out from New York to the ambulance service in Italy, he would continue the ruse of his love affair with Mae Marsh. He rattled his family with marriage plans and confided in one of his *Star* colleagues that he blew the cash his father had given him on an engagement ring. "Miss Marsh no kidding says she loves me," he would tell Dale Wilson in May. "I suggested the little church around the corner but she opined as how ye war widow appealed not to her." Decades later Wilson finally did what any reporter worth his salt would have done: "It took me forty-eight years to finally get in action and check the accuracy of that engagement. I phoned to California in 1966 to Mae Marsh, the movie queen of *The Birth of the Nation.* 'Yes,' she said she had been in New York in 1918, in fact had married Lee Armes, still her husband, there in September, that year. 'Did you ever meet Ernest Hemingway?' 'No,' she said, 'but I would have liked to.' It would seem that Reporter Hemingway in that 1918 letter was trying out his fiction writing on us back in Kansas City."

Dale Wilson was one of the "swell bunch of birds" who surrounded Hemingway in the newsroom, a bunch of guys who rivaled his gang back home, he told Marcelline. Wilson—"one of my best pals here"—was headed north to become a radio operator, and Hemingway prepared the way for a possible visit. She should treat him well and would soon discover that "he is a heller of a good feller and will tell you all about the greatest of the Hemingsteins." Wilson was fond of Hemingway's spirit and forever fascinated by the wordplay with which he engaged his new, mostly older colleagues. To Hemingway, Wilson was "Wilse" or "Woodrow Junior." He also experienced Hemingway's streak of combativeness. "He bristled at injustice. A bully at a lunch counter one Saturday night belittled 'Lovely Leo'"—the "smartly dressed" fellow staffer Leo Fitzpatrick. "Hemmy swung at him, missed and smashed a showcase. His bandaged hand was his hero's badge. He would modestly explain that it was nothing." (Here is another junction where a myth collides with reality, where memories conflict and stories about the eighteen-year-old nobody from Oak Park begin to grow bigger than life. Carlos Baker recounted that story in his monumental biography of Hemingway in 1969. A few years later, Marcel Wallenstein, a contemporary of Hemingway's at the *Star* who went on to become a foreign correspondent, batted the tale back. Hemingway wasn't at the diner that night, Wallenstein wrote, but Wallenstein was, and he witnessed Leo Fitzpatrick whipping the offender himself.)

Despite Hemingway's reputation for combat, Wilson sensed a bit of insecurity in the young cub: "There was a certain timidity in the Hemingway I knew. To cover it he put on the take-charge talk." Carl Edgar also testified to Hemingway's bravado. Along with becoming an "apostle of the violent" that year, Hemingway was "very aggressive and opinionated," his older friend recalled. Hemingway "could be and still can be vitriolic." And he was "very young, tremendously energetic and inclined to violence of opinion." Hemingway, however, projected a softer image more often than not and expressed a sweet fondness for his Kansas City pals: "They are all abit to the wild but a peach of a gang." Edgar and Hemingway got the benefit of "Ma Hemingstein's" cookies as her packages of food arrived from time to time. "I and Carl both are overjoyed when a box comes in," he told his mother. Cookies, tea cakes, vaudeville, and murder. The young man from Oak Park had a lot to be thankful for.

THE WAR BECKONS

I can hear you rave, but the Kid brother, while a mere infant,
has been out in this old sphere considerable lately.
And has seen many and various types.
Also he has had many and varied experiences,
it is the truth for a fact.
—HEMINGWAY TO HIS SISTER MARCELLINE

Ted Brumback had heard the shriek of shells, had carried the dead, had felt the jostle and horror of war. He spent nearly six months in 1917 driving ambulances in the French war zone before returning to Kansas City in November. By February 1918, he had convinced his new friend Hemingway that enlisting in the ambulance service would be a wholly plausible way to serve. Both of them had failed optical tests, which prevented their acceptance in the US military. The US Army had taken over the ambulance operation of the American Field Service the previous fall, so Brumback suddenly became ineligible to continue. Then, over the winter, the American Red Cross began sending ambulance men to Italy and issued an announcement that it would recruit more drivers. The *Star* even reported one Sunday that a former Kansas Citian had been accepted for an administrative role with the Red Cross ambulance corps in Italy after being rejected by the army.

As this idea stirred, Brumback sat down at a typewriter and poured out another memory of his bomb-shelled stint in France. The *Star* had published a letter from Brumback to his father the previous summer. In that item, he had described a night of action on the French front and "a most frightful bombardment" by the Germans. Brumback had also told pieces of his tale to the newspaper and in speeches to civic organizations. But now, Brumback delivered an all-out narrative of his experience. It amounted to some four thousand words in a Sunday feature section. And it got a treatment Hemingway never achieved: Brumback's initials, T.B.B., appeared at the very end. One could well imagine Brumback sharing with Hemingway the sheets as they came out of the typewriter or talking it all out over glasses of Chianti at Pecoraro's.

The story begins with a shift change. Brumback is sleeping upright in his ambulance, a respite interrupted by a call to head out. His is among a group of six vehicles parked in the square of a ravaged French village, a disturbing scene of destroyed slate roofs. Brumback eyes a ruined stone and plaster structure, "not much as a house, but the fine wine cellar in the basement provided shelter against the nightly marauders of the air." It's 2:30 AM. And in the dark stillness, Brumback learns the French are expecting another German bombing attack sometime before dawn. The incoming attendants had delivered "their sad burden of wounded" to the hospital up the street. One of them wished Brumback good luck on his shift. "Although this last was said with the best intentions, it grated on my nerves. I had heard stories about British soldiers who cursed anyone wishing them good luck just before they went into battle. I felt somewhat the same way." Brumback wakes up his partner, Tom Allen, and soon, "after two or three sputters and false starts," they head out of the square into darkness and uncertainty. It isn't dark and quiet for long. Searchlights eventually lace the night sky:

"It's a boche plane," Tom whispered, and at the same moment we caught the purr of a distant motor. Machine guns everywhere were now sending a storm of bullets skyward.

"Let's get out of here," I said, nervously, and the words were hardly out of my mouth before we heard a shrieking, banshee howl, followed immediately by an air-shattering explosion. "Bombs," Tom exclaimed, "and that one wasn't any too far away." "Just down the street," I said, pointing to the smoking ruins of a house across the way. In my excitement to get off I killed the motor by a too hurried start. "You idiot," Tom exclaimed, hoarsely. "Do you want to wake up with a wooden cross over you and somebody pattin' you in the face with a spade?"

He made several unsuccessful attempts to start the motor. "Let's run for shelter and wait till the raid's over." As I spoke the earth shook with a terrific explosion. I dived under the car, followed a close second by Tom.

Bang! Bang! Bang! Rocks and debris hit the top of the car. I ducked my head, coughing and choking, trying not to breathe the dust. Two more explosions followed in quick succession and then all was quiet.

"Are you all right, Tom?" I inquired, anxiously.

"Sure," came the cheery rejoinder. "But I'll bet the old 'bus is a heap of junk." He crawled from underneath and stood erect.

"Well, I'll be damned." He pointed to the driver's seat. Just where my head had been a few moments before was a jagged hole in the wooden body.

"And that's not all," he continued.

"How far do you think we can go with a hole clear through two cylinders?"

Racing With Hun's Shells

An Experience Running a Car "Over There" Described by an American Ambulance Driver

YOU'RE out next." I awoke with a start from a semi-doze. I had fallen asleep on the front seat of my ambulance. My driving partner, Tom Allen, was sleeping peacefully on a stretcher in the back of the car.

I stepped down and walked over to the boys who had just come in. They had backed their car in place alongside the five other ambulances standing in a line in the moonlit square of a little ruined French village. Their night's work was over. Their sad burden of

and see what had happened. About twenty-five feet away, up the street, was an almost symmetrical hole of about three or four feet in diameter and two feet deep. This had been made by a small bomb, else we never should have lived to tell the tale. Another had found its mark on a housetop about one hundred feet from where I was standing. The roof was completely demolished, but the walls remained intact. In the bright moonlight I could see smoke issuing from the ruins. This deserted village, a mass of ruins, was a

In February 1918, Ted Brumback produced a long narrative based on his ambulance corps stint in France in 1917. Shortly thereafter he and Hemingway applied to join the Red Cross to serve in Italy. *Kansas City Star*

Tom Allen, a "clean cut young American of about 20, with all the boy's feverish activity and thirst for adventure," returns to the village to pick up another vehicle. Brumback inspects the wreckage. The bombing left holes three feet wide and two feet deep in the streets. The deserted town suffers more collapsed roofs, and the smoke spiraling upward fills Brumback "with a sense of awe." After Allen returns with another vehicle and begins driving into the woods, he tells Brumback, "I have a hunch we're going to see a little fun tonight."

The drive through the woods is uneventful, and Brumback welcomes the moonlight and the quiet. The first French dressing station they encounter—a "*poste de secours*," Brumback informs his readers—is a complex of logs and sandbags. They stop but are sent to another outpost to pick up four wounded soldiers. A French officer greets them: "*Vous etre en retard* (you are late)." A surgeon warns that one of the wounded is in very serious shape.

Swathed in bandages almost to his eyes I could catch a glimpse of the man's face, pale as death itself. Over him was thrown a light, white woolen blanket, stained a dark mottled red just over his chest. At his feet lay a blue overcoat with three gold bars on the sleeve. A captain. With the utmost gentleness he was lifted into the car. The other three were already in.

We jumped into the driver's seat. It was Tom's turn to take the wheel. I was just stepping out in front to spin the engine over when there came to my ears that terrific whining drone, ominous and dreadful, that told of the approach of a shell. Instinctively I fell on my face in the road. With a hideous roar it passed overhead, exploding instantly some way down the road. I picked myself up only to fall flat again as another came over and burst in the same place. Two more followed in rapid succession and then hell seemed to open and let fly on us those unearthly, screeching devils. Swish, swish, roar, crump, announcing a big one, followed in unbelievably rapid succession.

I heard Tom calling, "My God! The Germans have started their attack and we're caught in the barrage. . . . We've got to get out of here and be quick about it. Hear the poor devils moaning inside. They know what's going on and they know they'll all be killed if we keep the car here much longer."

Nearly in panic, Brumback cranks the car and barely gets in as Allen speeds away. The shelling continues, sending "whirring fragments flying in all directions with terrific force." They pull up and stop before reaching a dangerous crossroads and decide to detour over a corduroy road through the woods. Brumback fears for the patients behind him, and he's grateful as he hears French gunners responding to the Germans' barrage. In the woods Brumback's "nerves were now worked up to a state bordering on frenzy." He hangs onto the side of the car and clenches his teeth "to keep from crying aloud." Tom Allen's face is calm and his hands grip the wheel. "Suddenly my eyes began to smart and my nose to tickle," he writes. "At first I did not pay any special attention, but the smarting sensation increased and I felt a grip at my lungs as if someone were trying to strangle me. In a flash it dawned on me; we had run into gas."

Brumback had not experienced it before, "this terrible invisible thing." He and Allen help put gas masks on their patients, even one who appears to have died. Before they continue on, a French soldier arrives, asking if Brumback and Allen can haul his wounded lieutenant. The ambulance is full, Brumback tells him, but Allen suggests the new patient could replace the one who had died. When secured in the back, the French officer speaks up. "Do not worry, *mes camarad.* . . . I am not hurt to the death. The thought that I ride with my American brothers shall cheer me and keep me from suffering. You come like angels from paradise to take me from this hell."

Brumback says he was nearly speechless. "Words like these make one feel he has done a service that is appreciated." Twenty minutes later, Brumback and Allen unload their patients. The "hideous night" is over. The morning sun is welcoming. "Everything was quiet and peaceful. I felt a warm exhilaration of pleasure. This was a life worth living, this soldier's life."

It's conceivable that Hemingway listened intently to Brumback's words and even choked up as the French officer thanked the "angels from paradise" delivering him from hell. Brumback's account was vivid, direct, passionate. It gave a strong picture of the kind of experience Hemingway might expect as he headed to the Italian front in the coming months. Brumback had faced death; he'd survived gas and the relentless downpour of shells. And then he wrote about it so thrillingly. Oh, perhaps there were a few too many adverbs, but Brumback could tell a story. And what a model of service. What a bond Brumback had formed with his story, and what a gift he gave to his friend Hemingway—the idea that he could fight through any fear and live to tell about it, too.

On February 22, the *Star* published an item about the Red Cross's search for ambulance drivers, specifically for four men to serve in Italy. Some Hemingway biographers assert that Hemingway and Brumback intercepted a wire story and applied before the story ran. Yet Ernest told Marcelline in a letter a few days later that the inside information came from his own interview with Red Cross recruiters, probably Dell D. Dutton, the Red Cross director for Kansas City and Jackson County. "He learned that the Red Cross was only accepting men who were not eligible for the United States Services and the draft. They took men in general good health who were unable to fulfill the physical requirements of our own country's armed services. 'Could a man with poor vision in one eye get in?' he asked them, he told us later. The Italians answered in the affirmative."

As it turned out, 205 people responded to the Red Cross call. Although Hemingway and Brumback were not chosen for the first four or five slots, they learned from the Red Cross personnel unit in St. Louis that they would be on call if more men were needed. So it was yet unclear when exactly Ernest would head overseas. "I enlisted for immediate service but got gypped on the immediate end of it," he told Marcelline. Hemingway implored his sister to keep quiet about his plan. But he told her what he was expecting:

an Italian officer's uniform, a rank of first lieutenant, expenses paid, and more. "I now study French and Italian and have learned to drive an ambulance. right jazzy. Pull for the old bird."

Hemingway's application to join the Red Cross may have gotten a fraudulent push from any number of friends. There are tales that Wilson Hicks memorized the eye chart and fed it to Hemingway. Another journalist, Julian Capers, a drinking buddy who worked for United Press, provided an affidavit that swore Hemingway was twenty-one and spoke fluent French and Italian. A dozen years later, Hemingway apparently tried to return the favor. Capers had mentioned his desire for a news service posting in Paris or elsewhere in Europe. Hemingway offered to swear to Capers's skills in French. Capers demurred. "Thanks for your affidavit offer," he wrote, "but I believe I'd be safer really to know my stuff this time; they're not so careless about those details as they were during the war."

———————

As the foreign ambulance service loomed, Kansas City's faulty ambulance service at home was blamed for untimely deaths. Six-year-old Genevieve Latimer waited eighteen hours for an ambulance to take her to General Hospital. On February 2, she became the sixth meningitis fatality in a month and eighth overall in the city. A hospital investigation was trying to determine the cause of the delay, and a clerk refused to tell Hemingway, the reporter, whether the family's call had been given to an ambulance driver. It was more fodder for the Star's—and Hemingway's—campaign to keep the heat on hospital officials.

Hemingway's hospital coverage was leading to palpable rancor. As he boasted to his mother one day, the General Hospital's manager barred him from the building, apparently because of his

After he and sister Marcelline graduated from high school in June 1917, Hemingway posed with his siblings at the family home in Oak Park. *Marcelline Hemingway Sanford Collection, courtesy of Ernest Hemingway Foundation of Oak Park and the Oak Park (Illinois) Library*

Clarence Hemingway drove part of the family up to Walloon Lake for the annual summer vacation in Michigan, 1917. After a five-day journey, they stopped to visit with relatives in Charlevoix. *Marcelline Hemingway Sanford Collection, courtesy of Ernest Hemingway Foundation of Oak Park and the Oak Park (Illinois) Library*

Hemingway (right) spent part of the summer working his family's potato fields and apple orchards and haying with neighboring farmer Warren Sumner. *Marcelline Hemingway Sanford Collection, courtesy of Ernest Hemingway Foundation of Oak Park and the Oak Park (Illinois) Library*

LEFT: Hemingway learned how to fish early on and turned it into a lifetime pursuit. He caught plenty over the summer of 1917. *Photographer unknown. Ernest Hemingway Collection, John F. Kennedy Presidential Library, Boston*

RIGHT: The Hemingway family cottage, known as Windemere, sits along the shore of Walloon Lake in northern Michigan. *Photo by Steve Paul*

William Rockhill Nelson built an Italianate, tapestry-bricked headquarters for the *Star* at Eighteenth Street and Grand Avenue just a few years before Hemingway arrived. Nelson, an architectural hobbyist, directed the design to be patterned after the famed McLean House in Washington, DC. *Jackson County (MO) Historical Society*

The atmosphere of the *Kansas City Star*'s large, open newsroom during Hemingway's apprenticeship was not much different than this scene from the 1920s. *Kansas City Star*

Downtown Kansas City in Hemingway's day bustled with vehicles and people. This view of Walnut Street looks north from Tenth Street. *Missouri Valley Special Collections, Kansas City Public Library, Kansas City, Missouri*

LEFT: A *Kansas City Star* portrait of Hemingway as it appeared in a family scrapbook. *Marcelline Hemingway Sanford Collection, courtesy of Ernest Hemingway Foundation of Oak Park and the Oak Park (Illinois) Library*

RIGHT: The newspaper's staff artists converted all photographs to line etchings. This one, signed "Tom," by Tom Douglas Jones, was used with a story about Hemingway's departure to Europe and again when the former staff member was wounded. *Kansas City Star*

LEFT: Hemingway, with the Sam Browne belt he picked up in Paris, sat for a formal portrait. *Ernest Hemingway Collection, John F. Kennedy Presidential Library, Boston*

RIGHT: Hemingway returned to Oak Park from Kansas City in May 1918, prompting a round of family snapshots, including this one with sister Marcelline. *Marcelline Hemingway Sanford Collection, courtesy of Ernest Hemingway Foundation of Oak Park and the Oak Park (Illinois) Library*

Carl Edgar, Charles Hopkins, and Bill Smith, all heading for various branches of military service, joined Hemingway (second from right) in Oak Park in May 1918 to make a fishing trip up north. *Marcelline Hemingway Sanford Collection, courtesy of Ernest Hemingway Foundation of Oak Park and the Oak Park (Illinois) Library*

Aboard the *Chicago*, a French steamship, as it crossed the Atlantic. Someone had coaxed the humorless French barman (left) to join the group photo. *Photographer unknown. Ernest Hemingway Collection, John F. Kennedy Presidential Library, Boston*

Hemingway (second from right) and his friends in the "Schio Country Club" made a sport of gathering enemy souvenirs. *Milford J. Baker Collection, Princeton University Library, Princeton, New Jersey*

Second-floor sleeping quarters of the Section 4 ambulance unit's barracks in Schio, Italy. *Milford J. Baker Collection, Princeton University Library, Princeton, New Jersey*

Hemingway posed in one of the Red Cross Section 4 ambulances, but he didn't spend much time driving one before he volunteered to join the rolling canteen service in order to see more action. *Ernest Hemingway Collection. Photographs. John F. Kennedy Presidential Library and Museum, Boston*

Amid the ruins of an Italian town, the graffiti reads: "Better to live a day as a lion than a century as a sheep." *Ernest Hemingway Collection. Photographs. John F. Kennedy Presidential Library and Museum, Boston*

In a letter to a friend, Hemingway said he "crawled out over the top this afternoon and took some darby pictures of the Piave and the Austrian trenches." This is very likely one of his photos. *Ernest Hemingway Collection. Photographs. John F. Kennedy Presidential Library and Museum, Boston*

American Red Cross recruits worked alongside Italian soldiers at the Piave River. *Library of Congress*

Like Hemingway, canteen workers delivered chocolate, cigarettes, postcards, and coffee to Italian soldiers in the trenches. *Library of Congress*

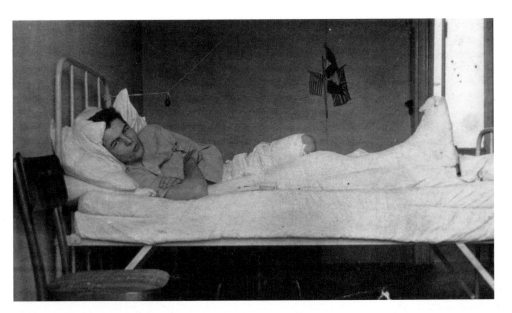

Hemingway recovered from his wounds for several months in the American Red Cross hospital in Milan. *Ernest Hemingway Collection. Photographs. John F. Kennedy Presidential Library and Museum, Boston*

Just outside the town of Fossalta, the Piave River bends near the location of Hemingway's wounding on July 8, 1918. *Photo by Steve Paul*

In 1979, Amici di Comisso, an organization devoted to the Italian writer Giovanni Comisso, who fought during World War I, raised a monument in Hemingway's honor above the Piave River at Fossalta. *Photo by Steve Paul*

aggressive reporting. "We are panning the hide offn them for fair," he wrote. Hemingway was proud that his boss kept sending him out "to get the dope on them." So much was going wrong. The contagion wing was always overcrowded. A doctor misdiagnosed a hospital cook with a rash before another determined he had smallpox. At one point, doctors were unable to order X-rays for seriously injured patients because the hospital had failed to secure a new supply of developer chemicals, and the business manager had nothing but excuses. One *Star* story, probably written at least in part by Hemingway, questioned the hospital and health board's accounting and hiring and firing practices, suggested that the hospital's business manager "has had no training whatever in public health matters," and accused a health commissioner, Dr. Eugene Carbaugh, of unexcused absences while he practiced privately in his uptown office. "Things are unbelievably rotten," Hemingway told his mother. By the end of April, before Hemingway left town, the young cub reporter would have the satisfaction of witnessing a hospital housecleaning, including the ouster of the business manager and Commissioner Carbaugh.

Kansas City's drug problem continued unabated, and in early February another strong rebuke arrived from the War Department. Its report on vice in the city, under investigation since November, withheld no punches. Clean up or else. H. R. Ennis, president of the board of public welfare, elaborated on the problem and put out an alarm in a public speech. The Municipal Farm was overpopulated with prostitutes, ex-cons, thieves, and crooks. "There are doctors with open offices who live solely off of drug using patients," and, despite a law banning the sale of heroin, cocaine, and morphine, a drugstore chain catered specifically to drug users. "This situation is horrible and there is nobody taking a hold of it," Ennis said. "There is no honest attempt by local authorities to suppress this illicit traffic." The *Star*'s editorial writers complained that "the shocking conditions Mr. Ennis recited will continue until the alliance between vice and politics, which has existed in Kansas City for many years, is broken." Ennis got into a spat with a criminal court judge over lenient fines and an inability to handle repeat offenders. Police officials contended Ennis exaggerated the problem and continued to defend the department's record of a crackdown on immoral resorts and narcotics. A federal narcotics inspector for the Internal Revenue Service backed up Ennis when he reported that drug trafficking in Kansas City was worse than every other city in the nation, except for New York and Boston. For Hemingway, it all was grist for the daily mill and for the churning consciousness that evolved toward its literary destiny.

————————

John L. Sullivan, the great pugilist and "one of the most picturesque characters in the history of prize fighting," died at age fifty-nine, and his obituary made page one of the *Star*. Following the recent deaths of Les Darcy and Bob Fitzsimmons, Sullivan's story was put in high relief for readers like Hemingway, who was an avid boxing fan and roughhouse slugger. The "Boston Strong Boy" knocked out "two hundred men of one sort or another in his fighting career," but seemed to be proudest of his triumph over the "black bottle," his decision in 1905 to give up drinking. Sullivan made much of the detail that he had earned $3 million in the ring and "spent 1 million of it in buying drinks for himself and his host of admirers." Hemingway, though, would have been more impressed by the mention of Sullivan's toughest encounter, the seventy-five-round epic bout he won over Jack Kilrain outside New Orleans. It was "the last championship contest in the United States to be fought with bare knuckles." Hemingway, when he boxed, mostly used gloves. Nevertheless, his bare-knuckled battles—with friends and others—would eventually become legend.

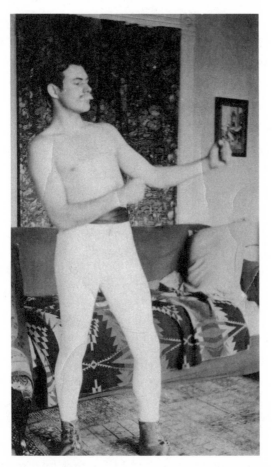

Hemingway put on a John L. Sullivan pose for his friends in Chicago, 1921. *Photographer unknown. Ernest Hemingway Collection, John F. Kennedy Presidential Library, Boston*

William B. Moorhead was the *Star's* police beat veteran, usually working out of the department's dingy headquarters in the North End. Moorhead was fearless and also hard-luck and humorless. Yet he was the kind of newspaperman who developed a sense that the crime and violence, corruption and despair he encountered and wrote about revealed something meaningful about the frailties of human existence. "He also sought among the routine police reports for a hidden phrase, sentence or situation which would reveal the droll, eccentric or unusual actions of men and women." In other words, he could be a perfect mentor to a beginner like Hemingway.

One day, Wellington sent Hemingway down to the police station pressroom at Fourth and Main. He was assigned to get some atmosphere. Laundry workers happened to be on strike, and police got the call that the workers were rioting, throwing rocks at a laundry. Moorhead called Wellington, who ordered them to the scene. Moorhead and Hemingway took a cab to Fourteenth and Euclid, a dozen or more blocks east of downtown. Moorhead recalled the day years later: "There were many strikers and few police. The rock barrage continued at intervals. Hemingway pointed out one of the throwers to the police, who shoved the man into a patrol wagon. The prisoner's friends lifted the wagon, bouncing it up and down. Several of the strikers then started toward Hemingway and me. 'Let's go!' I shouted. 'These cops can't protect themselves, much less us!' We ran to a street car and escaped as the crowd hurled stones at us. That was Hemingway's first baptism of fire."

One could quibble about how many "baptisms of fire" Hemingway had already experienced in his first four months at the newspaper. But once again being in the midst of action and danger gave Hemingway a rush. At Moorhead's pressroom, Hemingway also encountered the odd bail bondsman, lawyer, or cop dropping in for a round of poker or craps. "Hemingway didn't participate, but watched intently," one *Star* man wrote years later. But too bad for poor "Broken Bill."

The laundry strike, seeking higher wages and the right to organize, had been underway for weeks. As Hemingway and Moorhead fled the first scene, the melee at Fourteenth and Euclid expanded. As reported in the *Star* later that day, sympathizers overpowered a small group of special officers, hijacked a laundry truck, and drove it over the Cliff Drive hill. The truck was found later thoroughly demolished. More violence erupted periodically. A laundry guard riding along with a delivery driver was killed a couple of weeks later. Hemingway reported on that story and sent a clip to his father, who, given the details of a marauding "wrecking crew" and rampant stone-throwing and vehicle-smashing, must have felt a pang of concern for the safety of his son. A general strike, mostly involving streetcar workers, enlarged the labor action later in March. Riots erupted one day in various downtown locations, prompting the mayor to call in the Home Guard early in the morning of March 28. (There's no evidence that Hemingway was pressed into guard duty on that mission and no record of a conversation about the journalistic propriety of putting on a uniform in the midst of breaking news.) But pressure from antiunion business leaders and the American Federation of Labor, which had signed on as a way to support the war effort, led to a compromise in early April.

One day in mid-March, two cars carrying the Chicago Cubs pulled into Union Station behind the regular Santa Fe train, and Hemingway caught the assignment to meet up with them. The team was heading to its spring training camp in Pasadena, California. Waiting at the station to join the team was Grover

Cleveland Alexander, the pitching ace whom the Cubs had just purchased from the Philadelphia Phillies for $75,000. "Alec" wanted some dough as well and apparently was holding out for a $10,000 bonus, according to Hemingway's story. Hemingway talked with manager Fred Mitchell, Alexander, and several other players. He told his father that he bought Coca-Colas for "Alex and Pete Kilduff and Claude Hendrix," prompting the explanation that "drinks purchased to get a story are by order of the boss called car fare."

Unlike the laundry strike stories and the hospital reports, Hemingway felt free to dish out this sports story with a Lardneresque flair. He noted that although Alexander had yet to sign a contract, he checked his trunk for the full westward journey: "Grover Cleveland may not sink his fins into any portion of that $10,000 bonus he is demanding for attaching his monogram to a Chicago contract, but he isn't passing up any free trips to California." The "fins" and the "monogram" might not have passed the test presented by William Rockhill Nelson's aversion to slang, but Hemingway's editor that day had no trouble with it, even when Hemingway piled it on a couple of paragraphs later. He sounded almost as if he were still writing for his high school paper: "The guessing is now on as to what station along the route will flash the news that Grover Cleveland has ornamented a contract with his own peculiar style of hieroglyphics." Hemingway hung around for at least an hour and finally watched as the "Cub special, no accent on the special," pulled away, "cabooseing out of the station on the Santa Fe regular, with Manager Mitchell's right arm about the mighty 'Alec's' shoulder and his left patting the recalcitrant Kilduff on the back."

Mrs. Hemingway's cookies and cakes were always a hit. Another box arrived in early March, and Hemingway shared the treats among his friends in the pressroom at the Muehlebach Hotel. "The fellows all agreed that Mother Hemingstein must be some cook," he told her. "Your praises were sung in loud and stentorian tones. The cake sure fed a multitude of starving and broke newspaper men tonight." Hemingway's always cheerful, perhaps stentorian friend T. Norman Williams, known as Tubby, recalled the night for its "celebrated feast of fruit cake and cookies in Mr. Muehlstein's press house—that noble temple of temperament that was desecrated and turned into a den of iniquity." The nights probably ran together for Williams and Hemingway, but perhaps that night was not unlike the night Williams once recalled when Hemingway "soothed my burning brow or firmly held my splitting dome whilst my mouth, responding to the demands of a perturbed and abused stummick," heaved "upon Mrs. Muehlstein's immaculate press house floor." Hemingway's dutiful countenance toward his mother, often masking his youthful escapades, held steady throughout his apprenticeship, even as he put in the countless hours chasing stories and hitting the town at night with Ted Brumback, Tubby Williams, and others. With the ambulance service looming, Hemingway could sense that his days in Kansas City were numbered.

11

"SNAP AND WALLOP"

I have had a lot of valuable experience and have done some good work
and have hit it pretty blame hard. And now Pop I am bushed!
—HEMINGWAY TO HIS FATHER

One year after the United States agreed to shore up the Allied
war effort in Europe, mobilization remained a bit short of
Theodore Roosevelt's expectations, but the American presence on
the front lines had finally materialized. U.S. TROOPS TO BATTLE
was the prominent headline April 1 in the morning paper, its front
page almost completely devoted to the war. Hemingway felt himself in the thick of it. In late March he'd told his parents how closely
he and his fellow journalists were watching a German assault on
France. The routine of the newsroom involved smashing out stories,
then hopping up to check the wire machine for bulletins. In April
he wrote several stories about military recruiting. A year earlier, as
Hemingway was finishing high school, he had imagined himself
joining the army, a dream dashed first by his father and then by
his vision problem. Now his path to the war via the Red Cross
ambulance service had become clear. His friend Ted Brumback
had made that future palpable in their conversations and in the

narrative he'd written for the *Star* in February. And Hemingway's
sense of the war and the risks and sacrifices of other young men's
involvement became heightened the more time he spent with the
recruiters for various branches of the service. Roosevelt contributed to that sense as well in the pages of the *Star*. "It is these men
at the front who are now making all Americans, born and unborn,
forever their debtors," the single-minded former president wrote
in early April. "They are the men who have paid with their bodies
for their soul's desire. Let no one pity them, whatever their fate, for
they have seen the mighty days and have risen level to the need
of the mighty days. . . . It is a terrible thing that our loved ones
should face the great danger, but it would be a far more terrible
thing if, whatever the danger, they were not treading the hard path
of duty and honor." In the coming years—in his writing years, after
the war and as his thoughts about it matured—Hemingway would
have a different take on duty and honor. But for now, the kid from
Oak Park could certainly embrace it. To read his articles from this
period is to gain a close-up view of patriotism in wartime and of
the impulse, usually different for each individual, that sends a soldier eagerly into the fray.

   In one recruitment story Hemingway listed five Kansas Citians
and one Chicagoan who were chosen to join a new army tank
corps. A total of twenty men had gathered at the recruiting office
at Twelfth and Grand, six blocks north of the newspaper. "The
men of the tank corps enlist in a dangerous branch of the service,"
Hemingway wrote, "but it is thrilling work and, like aviation, has
long periods of rest and inactivity between the short, concentrated
spells of action." The enlistees would head for special training
at a camp near Gettysburg, Pennsylvania. Hemingway learned
from an officer what the six men could expect. His story reflected
the careful details and sensory facts that Hemingway would ever
employ. The gunners and artillerymen "crawl into the close, oily

smelling steel shells. . . . The tank lurches forward, climbs up, and then slides gently down like an otter on an ice slide. . . . The crew inside work the guns while the constant clatter of bullets on the armour sounds like rain on a tin roof. Shells are bursting close to the tank, and a direct hit rocks the monster. But the tank hesitates only a moment and lumbers on. Barb wire is crunched, trenches crossed and machine gun parapets smothered into the mud." Then the exercise is over and "it's back to barracks and rest."

The hard cadence of experience ("the smell of burnt oil, gas fumes, engine exhaust and gunpowder") and the figurative language (the tank sliding "gently down like an otter on an ice slide"), despite its clumsy "slides/slide" in the same sentence, prefigure Hemingway's war writing to come. For this feature story, Hemingway captured a choice quote in his interview with the corps recruiter: "'We want fighters for the tank service,' said Lieutenant Cooter today. 'Real men that want to see action. No mollycoddles need apply.'"

On the same day, five blocks away at Eighth and Walnut, Hemingway reported on a navy recruiting drive. Thirty-eight men were accepted, the largest daily total so far that year. In another story, the navy ordered that draft age office workers in the reserves, or "desk warriors," as Hemingway put it, be assigned to sea service. Hemingway wrote at least two more stories about recruiting for the tank corps. One of them was a full-blown narrative*, once again notable for its detailed, sometimes humorous descriptions and dialogue:

Four men stood outside the army recruiting office at Twelfth Street and Grand Avenue at 7:45 o'clock this morning when the sergeant opened up. A stout, red faced man wearing a khaki shirt was the first up the stairs.

---

*Reproduced in full in the appendix.

"I'm the treat 'em rough man," he bawled. "That cat in the poster has nothing on me. Where do you join the tankers?"

"Have to wait for Lieutenant Cooter," said the sergeant. "He decides whether you'll treat 'em rough or not."

The fat man waited outside the door.

Lt. Cooter's office proved to be a fount of feature stories. Hemingway gathered more material a few days later. He encountered a true character, a man of the world with adventures to speak of, and he spun another dialogue-driven narrative for the opening section of this story:

"Have you ever had any gas engine experience?" asked Lieut. Frank E. Cooter, special tank officer at the army recruiting station, Twelfth Street and Grand Avenue, yesterday.

"Well, you might call it that," replied William A. Whitman, 914 East Ninth Street. "I've driven a Blitzen-Benz at the Chicago, New York, Cincinnati and Los Angeles speedways for the last four years. You might call my race with Ralph Mulford at Reno a gas engine experience. Or the time the old boat got up to 111 miles an hour at the Sheepshead Bay track, or when Bob Burman was killed on the big board oval and I piled up right behind him. Those were gas engine experiences."

"But have you had any military experience?" asked Lieutenant Cooter.

"Well, not regular military. I held a lieutenant's commission in the Nicaraguan army in the war against Honduras in 1909. I was also a machine gun captain with Madero when he put Diaz out. First American to get into Juarez. Ask Pancho Villa, he knows. But none of those were very military. I had a commission in a couple of Central American revolutions, too. Nothing very military there, either."

Lieutenant Cooter shoved a blank toward him. "Sign on the dotted line, man," he said. "You're too good to be true!"

"Ernest was a boy when he was on *The Star*, just beginning to find himself," Henry Haskell, the editorial page editor and college friend of Uncle Tyler Hemingway, once recalled. "Nobody regarded him as a ball of fire, as a man with an undoubtedly brilliant future as a writer."

And yet Hemingway believed the fire had stirred in himself, and he would challenge that image of the apple-cheeked, innocent boy. In mid-April, two weeks after Hemingway and Brumback served notice that they'd leave at the end of the month, he poured out a passionate account of his apprenticeship in a long, stirring letter to his father. Clarence Hemingway had sent him a clipping from the Oak Park newspaper, in which the good doctor had made a reference to his son's accomplishment despite that he was merely eighteen years old. Hemingway took offense and told Clarence as much. But, sitting and somewhat seething in the Hotel Muehlebach pressroom, he went on to describe how he'd been "hitting the pace pretty blame hard" and holding his own while competing against older and more experienced men. Hemingway figured he'd crammed about three years of work in the last six months at the *Star*. Perhaps that was the speeded-up goal he'd set for himself after reading Richard Harding Davis's estimation of what could be accomplished in three years as a reporter. He was getting better assignments than some of his elders, and by way of "good luck and some natural ability I have been able to get into the game pretty well." He wasn't much happy with his seventy-five dollars a month and thought he could do much better if he moved on to St. Louis or Dallas or even Topeka. He was a fool to stay in Kansas City, his colleagues told him.

Hemingway, curiously, did not say a word to his father about the ambulance service and his pending, though still uncertain, deployment. Instead he laid it on thickly about the relentless hard work and how tired he was. He couldn't sleep, he was losing weight, he was "mentally and physically all in." Hemingway recognized the equivalency between the newspaper gig and the academic experience he'd chosen to skip, concluding that his exertion made it feel as if he were constantly cramming for an exam. Being absolutely accurate and responsible for the facts was stressful. Getting someone's middle initial wrong could lead to a libel suit, he said. In the middle of the letter, Hemingway winds up and pitches a blazing fastball, a concentrated bit of poetry in motion that sums up the cause of his exhaustion amid the clatter and tension of the news business as he found it: "Having to write a half column story with every name, address and initial verified and remembering to use good style, perfect style in fact, and get all the facts and in the correct order, make it have snap and wallop and write it in fifteen minutes, five sentences at a time to catch an edition as it goes to press. To take a story over the phone and get everything exact see it all in your minds eye, rush over to a typewriter and write it a page at a time while ten other typewriters are going and the boss is hollering at some one and a boy snatches the pages from your machine as fast as you write them."

Other people he knew would have gone wild, he said. Hemingway did not go wild. His assertion was that he had endured and even thrived. Yet he needed a vacation. He'd get home by May 2, he told his father, and then head north to Michigan with his friends Brumback and Charles Hopkins of the *Star*. And then he'd go wherever the news business called him. Again, no mention of ambulances or Italy or volunteering with Brumback. No mention even that he had given his notice, although that would have been implied in his plan to leave. Hemingway had told his aunt Arabell of his plan. She had even gotten her father, the lumberman and civic leader John B. White, to write a letter of recommendation to the Red Cross. But Marcelline apparently had kept quiet, and the word from Kansas City had yet to drift up to Oak Park. In Hemingway's practice, communications with the parents often confirmed that less was a lot better than more.

Despite his exhaustion, Hemingway didn't appear to let up during his last few weeks at the *Star*. One story in particular caused many of his colleagues to take notice and slap him on the back. As Fenton wrote, this story prompted "enthusiastic prophecies about the eighteen-year-old boy's journalistic future." Fenton characterized Hemingway's touch in the story as "wholly implicit; he avoided both sentimentality and cheapness." The piece was short, concentrated, and vivid, especially its first few paragraphs:

> Outside a woman walked along the wet street-lamp lit sidewalk through the sleet and snow.
>
> Inside in the Fine Arts Institute on the sixth floor of the Y.W.C.A. Building, 1020 McGee Street, a merry crowd of soldiers from Camp Funston and Fort Leavenworth fox trotted and one-stepped with girls from the Fine Arts School while a sober faced young man pounded out the latest jazz music as he watched the moving figures. In a corner a private in the signal corps was discussing Whistler with a black haired girl who heartily agreed with him. The private had been a member of the art colony at Chicago before the war was declared.

Three men from Funston were wandering arm in arm along the wall looking at the exhibition of paintings by Kansas City artists. The piano player stopped. The dancers clapped and cheered and he swung into "The Long, Long Trail Awinding." An infantry corporal, dancing with a swift moving girl in a red dress, bent his head close to hers and confided something about a girl in Chautauqua, Kas. In the corridor a group of girls surrounded a tow-headed young artilleryman and applauded his imitation of his pal Bill challenging the colonel, who had forgotten the password. The music stopped again and the solemn pianist rose from his stool and walked out into the hall for a drink.

A crowd of men rushed up to the girl in the red dress to plead for the next dance.

Outside the woman walked along the wet lamp lit sidewalk.

After a brief bit of explanation of how the event was organized, Hemingway continued the narrative:

The pianist took his seat again and the soldiers made a dash for partners. In the intermission the soldiers drank to the girls in fruit punch. The girl in red, surrounded by a crowd of men in olive drab, seated herself at the piano, the men and the girls gathered around and sang until midnight. The elevator had stopped running and so the jolly crowd bunched down the six flights of stairs and rushed waiting motor cars. After the last car had gone, the woman walked along the wet sidewalk through the sleet and looked up at the dark windows of the sixth floor.

The story, MIX WAR, ART AND DANCING, bears a close reading for several points that resonate in Hemingway's past and future.

Hemingway would have known of the Chicago art colony and indeed would have been aware of James McNeill Whistler's work through visits to the Chicago Art Institute and his mother's avid and accomplished avocation as a painter. As a woman who once wanted to become an opera star, Grace Hall Hemingway might very well have had a recording in her parlor of the Irish tenor John McCormack singing "The Long, Long Trail Awinding," a popular, plaintive love song of the day. It could be said that the whole scene—the dancing, the woman in the red dress, the solemn pianist, the jazz music, the jolly crowd rushing out at midnight, the melancholy prostitute—prefigures the feel and background of *The Sun Also Rises*, the Paris novel that lay seven or eight years in the future. The trope of the woman walking the street is a reminder that through his hospital and crime reporting and the narcotics epidemic, Hemingway became well aware of the sex workers who populated many blocks in and around Kansas City's downtown. Stylistically, Hemingway's repetition of the image of the woman walking in the sleet under the streetlamp— at the beginning, the middle, and slightly varied at the end of the story—would become a familiar, somewhat poetic device in Hemingway's future work. While most scholars and critics point to the future influence of the repetitive Gertrude Stein in Paris, another theory has emerged recently. H. R. Stoneback offered the unprecedented suggestion that Hemingway learned much from an important textbook on balladry and folk songs, which was introduced to the young, eager reader in the ninth grade. Line repetition is a staple of songwriting.

Finally, it is deliciously tempting to consider whether one of the soldiers from Fort Leavenworth one-stepping with the art students or perhaps discussing Whistler was Francis Scott Fitzgerald. He had left Princeton and, after arriving at the Kansas army outpost in November 1917, began feverishly writing a novel. This is mere fanciful speculation, of course; by April 1918, Fitzgerald might already have transferred to a camp in Kentucky. (Later that summer he would meet his future wife, Zelda Sayre, while stationed near Montgomery, Alabama.) But the timing of their midwestern experiences does prompt the notion, unverified by existing letters, that Hemingway and Fitzgerald must have discussed their shared and simultaneous history in Kansas City and environs. In a personal encounter some years ago with the radio reporter Susan Stamberg, she seemed to possess a bit of obscure but relevant Fitzgerald knowledge. Stamberg said that in an early printing of *The Great Gatsby*, Fitzgerald had somehow mistaken the name of the Seelbach Hotel in Louisville and called it the Muehlebach instead. She had indeed seen this very mistake, as that copy of the book was owned by a friend of hers with Louisville roots. If true, then Fitzgerald and Hemingway have one more shared link to Kansas City, given Hemingway's quality time in the Muehlebach's pressroom and his memory of the luxurious place, which he deposited, thirty years later, in *Across the River and into the Trees.*

As Italy lay ahead, Hemingway would have noticed news one day in April that an Italian officer would be making lecture appearances in Kansas City. Lt. Bruno Roselli of the Italian army told the City Club and other audiences about the dire conditions facing his people and his army. "Lieutenant Roselli said it was a wonder to him the soldiers succeeded in stopping the Germans at the Piave," the newspaper reported. "'Few people know our gunners were given only three shells a day and that our infantry depended on their bayonets and pocket knives because of their woeful lack of ammunition.'" As Hemingway's fictional

Nick Adams eventually told the Italian adjutant, "There will be several millions of Americans here shortly." And it wouldn't be long before Hemingway counted himself among those Americans doing their duty amid the Italian fighters and their foes along the Piave River.

12

"YOU SEE THINGS"

I don't want to flatter you, but I'd give a million dollars
in cold iron men if I possessed your originality.
—T. Norman Williams to Hemingway

Hemingway and Brumback picked up their last *Star* paychecks on April 30, and Hemingway prepared to board the Chicago train the next day. "Hemingway was delirious with excitement," Brumback said of his friend's sense of the next adventure. Kansas City had been very good to Hemingway. His friendships with Brumback and Carl Edgar had deepened. He had gotten what he wanted—a chance to prove himself as a writer, a path to independence from his family, an eye-opening experience of a city and its temptations, a sometimes grimy urban wonderland somewhat like a smaller version of Chicago. Hemingway left Kansas City with a boost of confidence. Some of it was self-contained, forged by his own impression that he had come and conquered. Some of it could be attributed to the kind words and cheery toasts from the chorus of newsmen around him.

Hemingway, of course, was a nobody as he departed the brick fortress at Eighteenth and Grand. To some he was still the "apple cheeked country boy," not very assertive, an innocent. "We recall that he used to express his determination some day to become a writer, but that is a determination often heard in newspaper offices," Henry Haskell told Fenton years later. Russel Crouse, the future playwright among the several developing literary talents at the *Star*, was somewhat more expansive: "Ernie, as I knew him, was a good reporter, not sensational by any means, and a completely nice guy. He came from Chicago which gave him some glamour in our eyes. I still believe that his simple narrative style came from the freedom of which he learned on the *Star*." The style sheet. Pete Wellington's gently demanding, corrective, and important guidance. George Longan's barking rebuffs. The impulse to be on the scene, to hightail it onto the rear end of an ambulance, to chase action for the thrill and the great pulse of a life force—all of that came together in Hemingway's Kansas City apprenticeship. Hemingway "learned the trick of credibility: a reporter had to appear authoritative, an expert on his subject," according to Michael Reynolds, and he embraced that kind of certainty as a way of life.

It's understandable that older veterans might not have seen the spark of greatness in Hemingway, especially years later as they sifted through memories and tried to reconcile the kid in the distant gray din of the newsroom with the celebrity who dominated American literature and the magazines. "He was terrible," said one distinctly grumpy and perhaps envious staffer. It was not uncommon to hear a story like the one Clyde Roberts used to tell on himself and his own experience when Hemingway's name came up in conversation:

And he proved how much I knew about writing. I was on police in those days, and it was close to deadline around noon when I phoned the desk with a pretty good story. Charley Blood was on the City Desk.

"I'll give you a rewrite man," he said.

"Who's on rewrite?" said I.

"Hemingway," he replied.

"Christ! Hemingway? He can't write."

Fenton interviewed many of Hemingway's *Star* colleagues and acquaintances in 1952, in the months before a groundswell of popular acclaim would erupt with the publication in September of *The Old Man and the Sea*. Five million copies of *Life* magazine! A book that captured hearts. Still, Haskell and the others surely had noticed as the sometimes awkward boy they once briefly knew progressed up the ladder of literary fame in the 1920s and '30s. The *Star* reviewed each of Hemingway's books. The reviews were not always favorable, but they reminded readers of his connection to the newspaper, and the *Star* frequently took note when its favorite son passed through town. But many of his contemporaries' memories were dim or insubstantial.

Those who were closer to Hemingway in the Kansas City period had a deeper regard for who he was and who he might become. Charles Hopkins, the night city editor, who sent him out on extra assignments and became a dear friend, told him, "Don't let anyone ever say to you that you were taught writing. It was born in you." Confronting that comment, Fenton concluded that Hemingway was "already too sophisticated in his trade to believe it."

The most significant testimony of Hemingway's talent comes from Tubby Williams, his fellow *Star* reporter. Fenton, while he worked on his study of Hemingway's early professional years, never found Williams. Tubby was "a most entertaining soul and very voluble," according to Bill Horne, who would meet Hemingway on the way to the ambulance service and Williams in Chicago after the war. A *Star* writer once wrote of him, "His specialties are being popular and noticeable." Roy Dickey agreed that Williams was "a glowing personality" and further identified him as the reporting peer who was "assigned the task of breaking Ernie in on the *Star*."

Given that perspective, Williams might have had the best view of Hemingway's development. Until Hemingway arrived, Williams was the youngest reporter on the staff, about twenty-two at the time, so they bonded well. Williams, a bit fleshy faced and double-chinned, came from a prominent newspaper family in West Plains, Missouri. He was among those who were duly impressed by MIX WAR, ART AND DANCING. By May 1918, Williams had moved on to the staff of the *St. Louis Globe*. In correspondence, he tried to tempt Hemingway with a job opportunity, but mostly he stroked the eighteen-year-old's burgeoning ego. Tubby's key letter arrived before Hemingway left Oak Park for New York on his way to the war in Italy. He addressed his "Beloved Hemingstein" and urged him to pack a typewriter and send stories back to the *Star*'s city editor, "the Great Longanbaum." If not, "you're just a plain damn fool":

This is your chance—the opportunity of your lifetime to make the limelight. You can do it. You can do it big. I don't want to flatter you, but I'd give a million dollars in cold iron men if I possessed your originality. You see things. You know things. You read human interest like a book. And above all you can tell it. All you need to do is to keep your confidence in the Great Hemingstein screwed up to the highest pitch. Six months or a year at the war game, writing stories on the side, will give you a leap of four or five years over the average young chap who goes into the great old game of journalism. It will be the making of you—the beginning of a career.

I'm happy to tell you, Hemingstein, that I never have seen a young fellow that I thought had the future in the news game that you have.

It will be the making of you. You see things. You know things. You read human interest like a book. And above all you can tell it. This is an astounding assessment of Hemingway, the fledgling writer, still green, not yet scarred by war. Tubby Williams was certain, maybe shared his friend's own certainty, that Hemingway would make a grand mark:

Your honors shall be my honors, for I shall be as proud of them as you and I shall not envy you. I just want you to do this one thing for me. Hit the ball and make good and then when you get to going good all I ask is that you remember that it was none other than the Great Tubstein (at that time the youngest man on the paper) who had faith in you and told you how it all would end. Then I can sit back with my cigar at a 45 degree angle and my thumbs in the armpits of my vest and say, "I told you so."

In the letter Williams gave Hemingway memories and greetings. Elizabeth Moffett already missed Hemingway, Williams said. Hemingway rarely failed to swing through her unit on the building's first floor, out of direct sight of the manly newsroom one flight up, on his way out of the building. Mother Moffett was a respectable, witty, and friendly substitute for his own mother. Hemingway confided in Moffett, though with about as much irony and deflection as with everyone else. Moffett recognized that he was a teller of tales and told Fenton that Hemingway had said "he left home because his mother wanted him to dress for dinner every night." Moffett also recalled how Hemingway had swooned over

Mae Marsh, the movie star, though she was silent on the issue of whether Hemingway actually met her, another point to chalk up against that notion. Juddie Hale, one of Moffett's staffers, loved Hemingway, too, Williams reminded him. Moffett said Hemingway was elated about going to Italy and had promised them a keepsake: "Mother, just as soon as I get my Italian uniform I'm going to send you and the girls (in the society department) a fevver (feather) from my hat."

Though some *Star* men assumed that Lionel Moise or Ted Brumback or both introduced Hemingway to Kansas City's brothels, it's more likely that he remained a sexual innocent. Sure he was aware of the tempting turf, and undoubtedly he encountered prostitutes in the course of his work and his play, but it's not likely that he followed through. Hemingway might have been telling his mother the truth in November when he said, "I havnt seen a girl," though he apparently never again brought up the subject to her, at least until he furthered the Mae Marsh hoax after he arrived in New York in May. To his sister, though, he was somewhat more revealing, if still wholly deflective. The imaginary Miss Marsh had bumped an Oak Park girl, Annette DeVoe, off the Hemingway pedestal of love, he told Marcelline. But other than Marsh, he never mentioned a Kansas City female friend to her—not Juddie Hale nor Sally Carrighar, a neighbor of Tyler and Arabell Hemingway, who once told Carlos Baker of a disastrous first and only date with Hemingway; not even Mother Moffett.

"He was feeling very grown-up to be so independent," Marcelline wrote later. "Instead of being older than he, I now felt younger, as Ernest's new experiences made him seem so much more a man of the world." Marcelline was impressed with her brother's ability to make friends, to be "congenial with people of all ages and from all backgrounds." Their father possessed that talent as well, she said. Though it was Ernest who "soaked up other people's experiences like a blotter," eventually sharing them "as his own." In that line Marcelline Hemingway Sanford might not have realized she was illuminating a truth about Hemingway's fiction.

Many readers still fail to understand that his books were not to be read as his biography. Fiction involves invention; Hemingway knew that above all and, in fact, learned the lesson quite well from the literati at the *Star*. If Hemingway's former colleagues made up tales about him, then so be it. Sometimes the life and the work were indistinguishable and sometimes not. Hemingway seemed to be happy about the attention either way.

When Hemingway left Kansas City, he and Brumback were still unsure of their Red Cross postings and of their plan. A preliminary notice soon arrived in Oak Park, and Hemingway sent a telegram to Brumback with word that he could go. He also had numerous questions about preparing for the eventual, though still unscheduled, journey to New York. "For a while," Brumback replied, "I was feeling rather blue, as I thought we would both be held up by red tape. How it came through so suddenly is beyond me."

Brumback told him that transportation to New York would be taken care of and the service would supply them with uniforms and equipment. Brumback said he'd bought an officer's trunk and advised against anything larger. He had also purchased winter and summer underwear, a half dozen pairs of heavy woolen socks, and both heavy and light sweaters. "Some of your Oak Park knitting bees ought to be able to fill this last order," Brumback said. Casting back to his ambulance stint in France, Brumback was quite specific about what Hemingway needed. Take your Seventh Regiment uniform, he said, heavy driving gloves, a couple of pairs of heavy shoes. A passport application was required, and Brumback told Hemingway to avoid a holdup and make sure that his would be sent to the passport bureau in New York rather than Chicago. Brumback's father urged him to read up on Roman history, "as a matter of preparedness." And he also took a stab at learning a new language. "I bought a little Italian grammar today am starting to work so I shall be able to order a bottle of Chianti in approved style."

Brumback regretted he couldn't join Hemingway in Oak Park for his planned fishing trip up north. Unlike Hemingway, he'd promised his parents that he'd stick around in Kansas City until the moment he left for Italy. Charles Hopkins, too, was wavering and uncertain whether he could get away. Hopkins, however, had just learned that the unit bound for Italy would leave May 15, Brumback said. Hopkins did manage to break away from work and join Hemingway in Oak Park for the fishing excursion. Hopkins eventually would take a navy post at the Great Lakes Training Station, not far from Oak Park, so he'd get to know the Hemingway family well that year. In one conversation with Clarence Hemingway, Hopkins predicted great things for Hemingway's future. "You could rely on that boy through thick and thin," he said, "or, as the army says, through 'hell and high water.'" Carl Edgar, who was bound for an army artillery unit in Kentucky, went along, too, as did Michigan buddy Bill Smith. The group boarded a train for Michigan. There was an urgency to that fishing break, a need for venting and for expelling the excitement of Kansas City while also stoking the fired-up expectations of what Italy, the ambulance service, and the war would bring.

After stopping at Horton Bay, Hemingway had his mind's eye set on making camp at a spot north of the Soo Line, the Minneapolis, St. Paul & Sault Ste. Marie Railroad, in Michigan's Upper Peninsula. At the last train depot the group made arrangements for the attendant to send an "Indian runner" if word arrived they were due to report to the Red Cross, according to Marcelline

Hemingway's somewhat flawed account, which she attributed to Charles Hopkins. Clarence Hemingway, now aware of his son's intentions, had promised to forward the incoming telegram, which was expected to arrive in Oak Park. If Hopkins was right about the May 15 departure from New York, then Hemingway and his friends had perhaps a good week or so in the woods ahead of them.

The Red Cross telegram did arrive in Oak Park within days. Hemingway's father received it on the afternoon of May 7 and immediately dropped a note and a transcript of the telegram (". . . proceed with passport application . . .") to Hemingway in care of the Dilworths at Horton Bay. The next day, another telegram showed up around noon ("Orders received to start men to New York"), and Hemingway's father forwarded its news again via James Dilworth. No telling where Hemingway was at the moment, but by the time the messenger reached the fishing party, they felt they had to decamp swiftly. Hemingway was forced to scramble his way back to Oak Park, where he'd barely have opportunity to gather his things and board a train to New York.

———————

Hemingway's train arrived in New York on Sunday, May 12. The next day he met up with Brumback, who had stopped in Chicago on the way from Kansas City and visited with Hemingway's father in Oak Park. The *Star* reported on the deployment of its two former staffers. Hemingway and Brumback would sail to Europe that very week, it said, though shortly thereafter the sailing date would be pushed back. Hemingway, prematurely identified as nineteen years old, "tried eleven times to get into service since the war started, but the physical tests ruled him out each time. He was a member of the 7th Regiment."

GO TOGETHER FROM THE STAR TO ITALIAN FRONT.

ERNEST M. HEMINGWAY   THEO. B. BRUMBACK

These two friends, one who has seen service in a French ambulance corps and the other who has made eleven vain attempts to get into different branches of the service, sail this week from an Atlantic port for Italy to join a Red Cross ambulance unit.

Theodore B. Brumback, son of Judge and Mrs. Hermann Brumback, and Ernest Hemingway, son of Doctor and Mrs. Clarence E. Hemingway, Oak Park, Ill., were members of the editorial staff of The Star. Brumback served the French from May to November, 1917, and was rejected from service for a physical defect which in no way interfered with his usual work when the United States took over the unit.

Hemingway, who is 19 years old, tried eleven times to get into service since the war started, but the physical tests ruled him out each time. He was a member of the 7th Regiment.

Two weeks after Hemingway left the newspaper, the *Star* reported that he and Ted Brumback would be heading to Italy and the Red Cross ambulance service within days. *Kansas City Star*

The Hotel Earle, a pair of nine-story brick towers attached to a three-story building at McDougal Street, stood a long block west of Fifth Avenue, overlooking Washington Square Park. Hemingway and Brumback took one of the Earle's tiny rooms together while awaiting their visas and passage on a French liner, the *Chicago*. Hemingway, Brumback, and some other friends explored the big city. They visited an aquarium at the Battery and traveled over much of Manhattan, from Grant's Tomb to the "Libber of

Goddesty," as Hemingway put it in a letter home. At the top of the Woolworth Tower, he watched camouflaged boats in the harbor and transport ships docked in Hoboken, across the Hudson. Hemingway's letter also itemized the contents of an officer's trunk supplied to each recruit in addition to the regular US Army officer's uniform ("1 officers overcoat $60 value. . . . 1 woolen shirt and a lot of other stuff I can't remember").

Then there was the matter of Mae Marsh, Hemingway's imaginary future bride. Now that he had an officer's uniform, he felt qualified to have her hand in marriage. To Dale Wilson of the *Star*, Hemingway went on about his passion for the actress, their frequent dinners, and the amount of money he was heaping on her ($150 for a ring). Hemingway implored Wilson to keep it quiet, perhaps a signal of his fantasy: "For God's sake don't let it get out amongst the gang and in the sheet." To his parents, Hemingway didn't use her name. He called her "the Mrs." and said he was scouting a church nearby. Just enough of a little nugget to put the scare in his folks. Clarence Hemingway wrote back to him immediately. "But please relieve our minds," he said. "A girl that marries a fellow of 18 or 19 seldom is at all satisfied with him when he is 23 or 25 yrs old. Never be ashamed to say no and to tell the truth." Clarence's letter appealed to the Hemingway family's Christian values and to his son's memories of love and bonding that he felt should override all else. He enclosed a picture of a rainbow trout to help Hemingway remember his summers at Walloon Lake. Hemingway swiftly responded. A telegram and Hemingway's confession arrived at North Kenilworth Street in Oak Park the next day. Just kidding—"not engaged married or divorced" and "me matrimonial status is negative and will be for some years." Carl Edgar, who had also received a letter from New York, essentially saw through Hemingway's "camouflage": "Where in Sam Hill do you get this Mae Marsh stuff?"

There were dances in New York, outings with Brumback to saloons, boxing events, drills twice a day, and long sightseeing drives with friendly society girls, who seemed to appreciate uniformed officers. Hemingway had dinner one night with Trumbull White, the editor and family friend who a year earlier in Michigan had encouraged his path in journalism. On May 18, Hemingway donned his uniform and joined a Red Cross parade of more than seventy thousand people down Fifth Avenue, a five-mile march along the spine of Manhattan, starting at Eighty-Fifth Street. President Woodrow Wilson led the proceedings for a couple of miles, then stepped onto the reviewing stand at Twenty-Third Street. At one point Hemingway found himself in the middle of Fifth Avenue, marching alone at the head of the Second Platoon and saluting the president as he passed. "I felt lonesome," he confessed to his parents later that day. It seems an odd thing to say for a gregarious young man having a jolly time away from home in the stimulating metropolis. ("Anything you want to know about N'Yawk ask me.") But being exposed like that, eyes right to face Woodrow Wilson himself and the thunder of war just ahead, gave Hemingway a moment of insecurity. By the time he wrote to Dale Wilson, his feeling had increased; he'd been "lonesome as hell." That might have been the only nugget of truth in Hemingway's account. As so often happened, Hemingway may have exaggerated his role, Steven Florczyk has noted. Hemingway was nowhere near the head of the parade, as he'd suggested, and was deep within a procession of dignitaries, Boy Scouts, nurses in a "human cross" formation, and many others.

––––––––––––

The steamship *Chicago* was a grungy old thing, "the rottenest ship in the world." Although several biographers assign a different departure date for the coal-burning French ship, the most logical, according to Hemingway's letters home, is Thursday, May 23, eleven days after he got to New York. The presence of Ted Brumback and Howell Jenkins, a short wisecracker with a red mustache, made the rotten ship endurable. And new friends emerged in the spirit of their shared mission. Some of them, including Bill Horne, a Princeton grad from Yonkers, New York, would remain loyal and devoted to Hemingway for the rest of their lives. To Horne, Hemingway was the "biggest and best looking of the whole outfit," about one hundred volunteers in all. "He was really a specimen of young manhood. He talked very well, using words of his own manufacture for many things and ideas and situations. It was fun to be around him."

Eighteen years later, Brumback recalled the journey in his article for the *Star*. The ocean passage was rather dull, he said, enlivened only by lifeboat drills and poker games. Hemingway had anticipated a thrilling night moving through a zone where a German U-boat had been spotted. In the end, when no such sighting occurred, "Hemingway felt he'd been cheated." (Hemingway would have another chance to scout for German submarines: during World War II, he outfitted his fishing boat to patrol the northern coast of Cuba, though once again, in their general absence, he likely felt cheated.) When it was discovered there was insufficient space on the lifeboats for the number of people aboard, Brumback was worried, but not Hemingway. "'What's the dif?' Hemingway said, patting his ancient life preserver. 'We've got as good a chance as those in the boats. They might get shelled anyway.'" Brumback and Hemingway killed plenty of time in the bar:

The monotony of the trip made us forget our fears. There was nothing to do but play poker in the bar, where a game went on day and night, or shoot craps. Here you had to be a quick thinker, for you were apt to be "covered" in French, English, Belgian, Italian, or American money. Hemingway tried it but found he was behind, although he won. There was no way to beat it.

The barman was an angular Frenchman with a walrus mustache who spoke English with a cockney accent. He interested Hemingway. At the first life boat drill he brought him on deck, protesting, where he was photographed with us. The barman had no use for the drills. Neither did we after the first one.

Hemingway omitted scenes like that in his shipboard letter to his family. He wrote about the weather, including pleasant breezes that reminded him of Walloon Lake. He conceded bouts of seasickness, though possibly attributed to the food on board. Lining up for a meal, he wrote, "I would se my next door neighbor clap his hand to his mouth and make a sudden break for the door and then the power of suggestion would be too much and I would break for the rail." Then again during two days of pitching and rolling during a storm, "I heaved but four times." Inoculations against typhoid also knocked Hemingway hard.

After his summers on the Michigan waters and excursions on the Des Plaines River near Oak Park, Hemingway enjoyed standing on the spar deck and gazing out at the ocean. "It is very good to look upon at night when the phosphorescent waves break out from the bow," he wrote. "The wake [i]s also a welter of phosphorous and when it is rough the crests of the waves will blow away lookinh like brands from a camp fire." These lines of close observation—he also reported seeing porpoises and flying fish—anticipate the Hemingway of the not-too-distant future. Indeed, Hemingway sketched a story about a night aboard the *Chicago*, eventually published as "Night Before Landing." In that short story, Nick Adams encounters two Polish lieutenants—Hemingway gives them character through dialogue and a scene that was missing when he mentioned the same men in the letter to his parents. Hemingway also recycled the imagery he'd captured while looking at the nighttime sea: "The water slipped softly, great patches of phosphorescent kelp churned out and sucked and bubbled under." And more: "They walked around the deck and down a ladder back to the stern to watch the wake phosphorescent and turning like plowed land in perspective." Hemingway originally conceived "Night Before Landing" as the beginning of a novel he wanted to call *Along with Youth*, a book undoubtedly meant to reflect his war experience. (A poem of the same title, which he wrote in Paris in the early 1920s, finds the writer reflecting on the decay of landscape and the past: "Drawers of boys' letters / And the line of love / They must have ended somewhere.") Hemingway discarded the novel early on, without getting much past the shipboard sketch that was published many years later. Nevertheless, the way the unfinished story resonates with the letter Hemingway wrote to his family aboard the *Chicago*, just a month after leaving his newspaper training in Kansas City, presents an indelible example of an emerging writer at work.

In "Night Before Landing," drinking ensues onboard the ship with Chocianowicz and Galinski, the two Polish officers. Yet because it is their last night at sea, Nick decides to forgo entering one of the spirited poker games underway in the bar. He is happy to drink wine and talk with Chocianowicz. That conversation reveals some of the fear Brumback alluded to. And when the Pole says he wishes they would "soldier together," Nick makes an odd confession: "I wouldn't be any good."

Florczyk explores the broad subtext about whether the ambulance service and other noncombatant roles in the war were considered inferior to serving in the military. Hemingway clearly was conflicted, and his Red Cross uniform was close enough to army garb that he could feel more important when he wanted to. In a few days, he'd buy a Sam Browne belt in Paris, a leather strap that made his uniform look even more impressive, though seasoned volunteers knew how superfluous and striving such a thing could appear. Yet, as the steamship approached Bordeaux, Hemingway, Brumback, and the rest of the ambulance recruits knew that their path to war and this adventure was both honorable and real.

Hemingway landed in France on June 3, the ship having steamed down the Gironde River past the bluffs of premier wine country. In Bordeaux, "all of us got high on the native product," Bill Horne later recalled. "Though honorary second lieutenants in the Italian Army, we were just kids, and getting half a bottle of wine into you was pretty serious business." The volunteers boarded the night train for Paris, where, Horne added, they "were received as persona grata" and "even saluted by French generals." Hemingway and Brumback reported to the Red Cross headquarters, on the Place de la Concorde, and took a room nearby. They stayed for not much more than a day or two. Hemingway made the most of it. Along with Brumback and Jenkins, he saw everything—Napoleon's Tomb, the Louvre, the Arc de Triomphe, the Folies Bergère ("Hot puppums," he announced to his family). Still, he thought Paris lacked the quaintness of Bordeaux. Nevertheless, he vowed to wander through the country once the war was over. In his brief experience, including conversations with the Frenchmen and chambermaids on the *Chicago*, he'd become expert at the language. "I have picked up a lot of French and can sling it pretty fast," he told his family.

Brumback's account of their arrival in Paris once again included details Hemingway left out of his letter home. Hemingway had told his parents about the sounds of Germany's infamous long-range guns that were resounding over Paris in random and unpredictably located bursts. "The people accept the shells as a matter of course and hardly show any interest in their arrival," he wrote. Florczyk finds that Hemingway's letter does an admirably journalistic job of prefiguring "dispatches he later wrote as a foreign correspondent and [indicating] an initial stage of development as a writer dealing with the effects of war." Brumback years later filled in some details, portraying the young Hemingway as eager for a thrill:

> When we arrived in Paris the Germans were shelling the capital with their long range gun, news of which had startled the world. . . . Hemingway was as excited as if he'd been sent on general assignment to cover the biggest story of the year. As we left the Gare du Nord we could hear the bursts from different parts of the city.
>
> "Come on, Ted," he said. "We're going to see something. Here, taxi."

Hemingway badgered Brumback and a reluctant driver into taking an excursion toward the explosions, "one of the strangest taxi rides I shall probably ever experience," Brumback wrote. Hemingway vowed to write about the adventure for the *Star*, though he didn't follow through. After an hour, they finally witnessed a shell striking the Church of the Madeleine and "chipping off a foot or so of stone. No one was hurt. We heard the projectile rush overhead. It sounded as if it were going to land right in the taxi with us. It was quite exciting. After that the Germans signed off for the day."

Despite Hemingway's boast to his family about his fluency with the language, it was Brumback who conversed with the taxi driver and translated Hemingway's pleadings. Brumback's French, honed by his time on the ambulance corps the previous year, clearly was superior to Hemingway's in that moment. Regardless, both of them were anxious to get out of Paris and get on with it.

13

AT THE PIAVE

I'm going to get out of the ambulance section and see
if I can't find out where the war is.
—HEMINGWAY TO TED BRUMBACK

I f Hemingway thought his entry to Italy would be a routine affair, with time to settle in and get oriented to Red Cross procedure and maneuvering over mountain roads, his expectations were upended almost immediately. The train from Paris had chugged through the Alps and into the Lombard valley past Lago Maggiore without incident. But not long after disembarking in Milan, Hemingway was called to duty. A munitions plant had exploded in a town a dozen miles outside the city. The horror of war unfolded before him in a field strewn with bodies and human remains. "We carried them in like at the General Hospital, Kansas City," he told a friend at the *Star*. Hemingway later reflected on the experience in "A Natural History of the Dead," a short story that he published both in a fiction collection and as a section of *Death in the After-noon*. "After we had searched quite thoroughly for the complete dead we collected fragments," he wrote. Hemingway pulled body parts from the barbed wire fencing that bordered the Sutter and

Thevenot factory. He seemed most alarmed that the fatalities were all women, the wartime employees of the Swiss-built operation. After returning to Milan, "I recall one or two of us discussing the occurrence and agreeing that the quality of unreality and the fact that there were no wounded did much to rob the disaster of a horror which might have been much greater." For Hemingway, then, to be wounded amid the carnage evoked greater horror than to contemplate the dead. Hemingway, according to the scholar Paul Smith, began writing "A Natural History of the Dead" shortly after his father, the doctor and natural historian, committed suicide in 1928. But at that moment, years before he wrote about the dead women in an Italian field and contemplated his father's embalmed body, Hemingway was still much the eager teenager, only partly seasoned by the scenes he'd encountered in Kansas City. The opening line of the postcard to his *Star* friend, the line before he mentioned his "baptism of fire," was this: "Having a wonderful time!!!" And he closed: "Oh Boy!!! I'm glad I'm in it. They love us down here in the mountains."

Hemingway, of course, hadn't been in the mountains long, but undoubtedly he was capturing a general spirit of enthusiasm among the Italians that the American forces had finally arrived. The Red Cross volunteers—the first wave had landed in November 1917—represented the promise of American military power to follow. The munitions-plant body-collection crew returned to Milan for a couple of days until the men received their postings. Hemingway and some two dozen others would staff one of five Red Cross ambulance sections in the region. He was bound for Section 4 in Schio. They traveled through the plains, along the southern edge of the Dolomite mountains, about 150 miles northeast of Milan.

The day Hemingway got to Schio, Austrians were shelling the town, according to Brumback's later account. Some places

supposedly were off-limits, by mutual agreement, or so everyone
thought. But the Austrians were aiming for the train station and,
once again, Hemingway got in gear, "running for the station to
get there before the next shell arrived." No such luck. "Visiting
team's started playing dirty ball," he said. "We'll hear from the
home team on that." And soon enough they did, the sound of an
Italian return volley piercing the air. Whether this was an early
display of Hemingway's wartime analytical skills or a hindsight
piece of hagiography by Brumback is a point to be debated.

The Section 4 recruits took up residence on the second floor
of a vacant, flea-infested woolen mill. Cots lined the walls of the
large open room beneath the high, big-beamed ceiling. A game
room beckoned across the hall. The first floor held the mess hall,
where Italian waiters served spaghetti and wine. A cold mountain stream gave the volunteers a place to bathe. The Dolomites
loomed in the distance, jutting out dramatically from the valley.
A field out front of the barracks was perfect for baseball games,
a recreational diversion that helped the camp earn the reputation
as the Schio Country Club. Another favorite activity was souvenir
hunting, and Hemingway did as well as anyone by collecting an
Austrian helmet and more. From one hunting trip, Hemingway
returned with an Austrian handgun and posed for pictures with
his fellow volunteers, six or eight of them lined up in helmets,
one blowing a bugle.

The Schio base was at the western end of the line separating
the Austrian and Italian forces, and the ambulances—seventeen
mountain-ready Fiats, model 25-35, painted gray—fanned out,
two men to a vehicle, to "cover our sector a little east of Lake
Garda, bringing in the wounded." Two or more Ford ambulances
in the garage were viewed mostly as capable of picking up grocer-
ies and mail. During the day, ambulance teams ventured up the
twisting mountain roads toward the front line, picking up patients

and returning to Schio. It remains unclear whether Hemingway ever drove that route himself or, if he did, how often. One image exists of him posing in the driver's seat of a stationary ambulance. In another postcard to a *Star* friend, Hemingway mentions he was "in the Alps riding in a Fiat"—riding in, that is, not driving—and adds that Brumback was in a Ford in the valley. In the evenings, according to Horne, the volunteers often walked into the town to revel at the Three Sisters Saloon and to make "friends with the people and try to talk Italian." Hemingway also liked the higher-class offerings at the Due Spadi hotel. He was surrounded by Ivy Leaguers, mostly older than him, and several of his Schio colleagues came from prominent industrialist families. In some cases those social differences made no difference, and he began several long-term friendships there.

In mid-June the Austrians began a one-hundred-mile offensive along the Asiago plateau, from the mountains to the sea above Venice. This was a long-expected campaign, an echo of the last Austro-German drive that began in October and crushed the Italian forces at Caporetto. Over the winter, fighting had begun again along the Piave River, northwest of Venice, and French and British forces had arrived to shore up the Italian resistance. Now, on the morning of June 16, a barrage of Austrian bombs erupted, followed a few hours later by infantry charges. The action came amid reports of severe political divisiveness in Austria and a populace hungry for peace, a situation exacerbated by the Italians' vigorous response. "Our troops are everywhere resisting magnificently," Italy's premier Vittorio Emanuele Orlando declared. Still, the struggle along the Piave continued. The Austrians crossed the river at some points, threatening to expand their reach. Yet, the Italian army seemed to maintain the upper hand. Soon bodies were strewn over the countryside, and the Allies took hundreds of prisoners.

At Schio, however, the ambulance crew had entered a lull. Hemingway was bored. "I'm fed up," he told Brumback. "There's nothing here but scenery and too damn much of that. I'm going to get out of the ambulance section and see if I can't find out where the war is." One day in late June, the opportunity arrived. Word arrived at Section 4 that men were needed to run emergency canteen operations for soldiers at the Piave front, where the battles and the shelling had become fierce. Horne and Hemingway were among those who raised their hands. Each would go to a different location behind the lines but much closer to the action. "They play ball down there," Hemingway said. "You're a fool," Brumback replied. "Everything's swell here."

Hemingway was sent to a sector near a crossroads between Fornaci and Fossalta, which was home to not a rolling kitchen as planned but a "rudimentary base without the benefit of a 'rest room.'" Less than ten days before, at the beginning of the Austrian surge, Lt. Edward McKey had been blown up at the same spot. McKey had been in charge of the sector and had intended to establish the canteen. He became the first American Red Cross casualty in the war. Michael Reynolds speculates that Hemingway might have known about McKey's death in that location when he sought to relieve his boredom in Schio: "It may have been chance that took Hemingway to the same sector, but he also may have gone at his own request."

Within days Hemingway was in Fossalta, a battered town just off the Piave River. The countryside between Fornaci and Fossalta was still sloppy with mud following a recent downpour and flooding. The soggy landscape was littered with the bodies of Austrian soldiers, evidence of the Italians' brutal rebuff of the enemy's charge. By one account, "It was an ugly sight; many of them had been dead for days."

The canteen supplied coffee by the cauldron, cigarettes, post-cards, chocolate, and other foodstuffs to the Italians in the trench, which, at Fossalta, lay about twenty yards from the Piave. Hemingway had settled into a two-story house in town; it had four rooms until the day an Austrian shell took one of them out, he told Ruth Morrison, an Oak Park friend. "Each aft and morning I load up a haversack and take my tin lid and gas mask and beat it up to the trenches," he wrote. He missed talking English with Americans and was "lonesome for the sight of a real Honest to Gawd American girl." Hemingway described sitting in a trench listening to the whimper and shriek of shells, the staccato of machine guns, and the all-night roar of the Italian guns. Hemingway urged Morrison to refrain from speaking about this with his family, "who fondly picture me chaufing a Ford through Sylvan glens."

Hemingway, rather than "chaufing" an ambulance, would pedal a bicycle from the house to the Italian trench. The Austrians were encamped just across the narrow river, beyond barricades of wood and wire on both sides. The Italian soldiers made perhaps two or three cents a day, so American cigarettes were "an impossible luxury," and to the troops, Hemingway seemed to be a personal representative of President Wilson himself. The Italians "got to know his smiling face and were always asking for their 'giovane Americano.'" On both sides of the river, sharpshooters took up posts in the tree branches. "I watched a clever Italian," Hemingway told Brumback. "He climbed a tree and lay for hours, motionless, watching the other side of the river through a telescope. At last he raised his rifle and fired. A body fell from a tree over there, clutching desperately at limbs while there was life. It reminded me of bringing down a mountain lion." At the time, Hemingway had probably not yet taken down a mountain lion, though undoubtedly he'd read about the experience. In any case, he had found the action he'd been seeking.

Hemingway spent barely two weeks in and around Fossalta, carrying out his daily duties and honing his skills as a witness to war. On quiet days he'd ride his bicycle and take pictures. On June 29, in a meadow not far away at Roncade, Hemingway heard the writer and airman Gabriele D'Annunzio deliver a speech to the Arditi, the famed mountain fighters; perhaps it was there that D'Annunzio, "his white face as white as the belly of a sole," uttered the line "*morire non è basta*" (dying is not enough) that Hemingway's fictional Colonel Cantwell recalls thirty years later in *Across the River and into the Trees*. On July 4, Hemingway celebrated the American holiday with Bill Horne, who was posted down the road in San Pietro Novello, in a barracks where Horne, if not Hemingway as well, heard the silkworms chewing at night.

Four days later, about midnight on July 8, Hemingway was perched in a dugout at a forward listening station near the river. From the other side of the Piave came a screech and a flash. An Austrian Minenwerfer bomb exploded three feet away. Between Hemingway and the mortar shell, an Italian soldier took the brunt of the blast and died, likely protecting the young American from extensive damage. Hundreds of metal shards ripped through the air and into Hemingway's legs. Brumback, after visiting Hemingway six days later in the American Red Cross hospital in Milan, described what he'd learned in a letter to Oak Park:

> The concussion of the explosion knocked him unconscious and buried him with earth. There was an Italian between Ernest and the shell. He was instantly killed while another standing a few feet away, had both his legs blown off. A third Italian was badly wounded and this one Ernest, after he had regained consciousness, picked up on his back and carried to the first aid dug-out. He says he does not remember how he got there nor that he had carried a man until the next day

when an Italian officer told him all about it and said that it had been voted upon to give him a valor medal for the act.

Carlos Baker, Hemingway's first full-length biographer, also depicted the moonless night, the sky "invisible except when the star shells climbed and broke in flowerings of white light." Baker attributed his narrative to the "most trustworthy account," a letter Hemingway wrote to his family more than five weeks later. In Baker's account, Hemingway was sweating through his tunic in the oppressive heat. He set his bicycle aside, near the forward command post, and went into the trench carrying the usual treats to the Italians. The soldiers expressed concern that the volleys of Austrian fire were alarmingly close. Then came a missile the size of a five-gallon canister, first giving off an eerie sound in the air, then unleashing its lethal metallic scraps at ground level. Baker relates Hemingway's rescue of the wounded Italian:

> His legs felt as if he were wearing rubber boots filled with warm water. Beside him was a man who made no sound. Just beyond him was another, badly hurt and crying piteously. Ernest groped for his neck and legs, heaved him up in a fireman's carry, and began to stagger back towards the command post. He had covered fifty yards when a round from a heavy machine gun tore into his right leg at the knee. It felt like an icy snowball. He stumbled and fell with the man on his shoulder. He never afterwards remembered how he had covered the final hundred yards. But he made it, delivered his man, and lost consciousness.

Steven Florczyk makes a detailed and convincing case that the story of Hemingway's heroism has long been exaggerated, most likely in the telling that begins with Hemingway himself. Red

Cross documents from those months of 1918 rarely mention that the wounded Hemingway hauled an Italian to shelter, and over time the reports appear to let the matter fade. "Indeed," Florczyk writes, "the final official chronicles had little to say about Hemingway as a hero." In late July, W. R. Castle of the American Red Cross wrote to Hemingway's father, reporting on a cable announcing the issuance of the Italian Cross of War to twenty-one ambulance drivers who performed "service of the highest importance" under the fire of an Austrian offensive. "The cable," Castle wrote, "goes on to say that your son was wounded while distributing relief to the soldiers in the trenches." There was no mention of Hemingway's supposed heroism.

In August, a Red Cross bulletin reported on Hemingway's wounding. It noted that he was recovering and notably added that he "had been commended for the way in which he conducted himself, having carried a wounded Italian some distance to succor after having been wounded himself." The final Red Cross report for the period, issued the following March, lamented the death of Lt. Edward McKey and listed Hemingway as one of thirty lieutenants who'd been in charge of various canteens. It went on to describe the qualities of these noncombatant leaders: "Courage and coolness under fire may also be mentioned as an attribute that these canteen officers were called upon to frequently display. One of these lieutenants was killed by an Austrian shell and another wounded in a front line trench while distributing supplies to soldiers." Hemingway was not named, and there was no mention of his carrying a fallen soldier back to safety.

Still, Hemingway may indeed have projected "courage and coolness under fire," and he certainly suffered aching wounds. Of 227 punctures, 10 or so were identified as serious, including bullet wounds to his right knee and foot. Hemingway took machine-gun fire as he left the trench, with or without a wounded soldier on his broad shoulders. Hemingway later implied that he'd "twisted a tourniquet" around his leg, "while the blood soaked your puttee and trickled into your boot, so that when you got up you limped with a 'squidge' on your way to the dressing station." In his letter of August 18, the account that Baker relied on, Hemingway never explicitly states that he carried a man on his shoulders, though he does suggest he helped a wounded soldier to safety: "The Italian I had with me had bled all over my coat and my pants looked like somebody had made current [sic] jelly in them and then punched holes to let the pulp out." Perhaps it is quibbling to wonder whether Hemingway had the Italian "in a fireman's carry," as Baker put it, or dragged the soldier, or helped him in some other physical way in between. What remains essential in Hemingway's experience on the moonless night at Fossalta was that at a crucial moment he imagined that he had felt his soul "go out of me and go off and then come back."

Hemingway was carried on a stretcher, first to the mayor's house, near the town's cemetery, according to one account, then to a roofless barn, to wait for an ambulance. "When it came I ordered it down the road to get the soldiers that had been wounded first," Hemingway wrote to his family. That moment of selflessness may well have earned Hemingway some valid attention. The shelling and artillery continued to shriek and boom through the night. At a dressing station, a *smistamento*, in a school building at Fornaci di Monastier, a surgeon administered morphine and extracted some splinters, and a priest quietly baptized him. Next stop was a field hospital near Treviso, where he spent several days of pain, uncertainty, and deep, groggy reflection, before being delivered to the Red Cross hospital in Milan.

Today, you can stand by the roadside above the banks of the Piave at Fossalta and see the green-tinted ribbon of water threading and bending along the flats. You can try to imagine where a mortar shell landed and pierced the body of a young man who wanted more than anything else to be a writer. You can read the inscription on a bronze marker, which honors Hemingway as he honored the place: Sono un ragazzo del Basso Piave. ("I'm a son of the Basso Piave" is how Hemingway would put it, embracing the terrain of the lower Piave Valley, which suffered so much during the Austrian attack and the fierce counteroffensive.) If Hemingway had a latent fondness for the place, he also had mixed feelings, which he revealed in later writings.

"Don't go back to visit the old front," he warned a few years later, in a dispatch for the *Toronto Daily Star*. In July 1922, four years after his wounding, Hemingway would take his new wife, the former Hadley Richardson, on an excursion from Paris to Schio and Fossalta di Piave. Schio was nothing like he remembered it. It seemed shrunken and offered nothing to reflect his feeling that it had been "one of the finest places on earth," because it had "all the good cheer, amusement and relaxation a man could desire" and represented the kind of wonderful place where one would want to "live after the war." Four years after his posting there, he would look "in shop windows at the fly-speckled shirts, the cheap china dishes, the postcards showing about seven different varieties of a young man and a young girl looking into each other's eyes, the stiff, fly-speckled pastry, the big, round loaves of sour bread." Perhaps by now Hemingway was in the process of shedding that old innocence, the action-adventure spirit with which he first embraced his wartime experience. "All the kick had gone out of things," he wrote. He'd become jaded.

Similarly, Fossalta had replaced "the shattered tragic dignity of the wrecked town" with a "smug, hideous collection of plaster houses" painted in ghastly bright hues. He would lament how "the change in everything and the supreme, deadly, lonely dullness, the smooth green of the fields that were once torn up with shell holes and slashed with trenches and wire, will combine against you and make you believe that the places and happenings that had been the really great events to you were only fever dreams or lies you had told to yourself."

Hemingway's startling confession here—if it can be read that way—begs examination. One could wonder what lies he had told to himself and perhaps others. The Hemingway journey is long and winding and full of contradictions as well as the eternal clash of fact and fiction. The interpretive problems posed by his invented self and the inventions of his later work have kept scholars busy for decades. He didn't help critics or students of his life and work by being clear about any of this. As Michael Reynolds once put it, "The misleading thesis that Hemingway is always his own protagonist has littered the critical landscape with so much debris that it will take another generation of critics to restore the ecology." In the years after the war, Hemingway let his publisher and others foster the notion that he had been a combatant in the Italian army. But he also from time to time tried to quash it or play down his supposed heroism and his receipt of the Silver Medal of Military Valor, which Italy gave him and only nine other men among the three hundred or so who served in the Red Cross ambulance units. But at eighteen, and in the months after, Hemingway was happy to be the center of attention, to elicit adulation for the sacrifice he'd made. "He was thoroughly spoiled by it," Hemingway's nurse in Milan recalled years later, but when he walked around on crutches in Milan, his uniform emblazoned "with his wound stripes and medals," he became the "laughingstock" among American soldiers. Robert Bates, the Red Cross ambulance inspector, was particularly disgusted by Hemingway. Florczyk suggests that Bates's close friendship with the fallen canteen worker Edward McKey made him sensitive to Hemingway's apparent disregard of the true hero of the Piave. "I not only did not admire him," Bates once wrote, "but knew him to be an incomparable braggart and liar!"

That was, perhaps, a harsh and emotional judgment, but based on the memories of some fellow ambulance drivers Bates was not alone in his enmity for Hemingway at his most immature. Yet, in the context of that war at that time, lying and braggadocio were all part of the fabric. As Celia Kingsbury has noted, "World War I was a war in which it was impossible to distinguish truth from lies." In the coming years, the innocent, brash, and immature young man would proceed to expand and burnish his emotional and intellectual being as he processed what he had experienced and injected those memories and inventions into a body of lasting literature.

––––––––––

After being unloaded at the Red Cross hospital in Milan, Hemingway was carried to a private patient room on the sixth floor. He was treated well, and the nurses fawned over him. In a week, he would turn nineteen. On his birthday, July 21, 1918, Hemingway penned a letter to his family. It even included a crude line drawing of himself, lying prone, legs bandaged over his 227 wounds, and exclaiming in a dialogue balloon, "gimme a drink!" Hemingway knew that his friend Brumback had filled the family in about the night at the Piave, and so he didn't elaborate, though he pointed out, incorrectly, that "I'm the first American wounded in Italy," forgetting about the fatally wounded McKey. With his doctor father in the reading audience, Hemingway described what X-rays showed about his condition and noted that the surgeon wanted to wait for the bullet wound in his knee to heal "cleanly before operating" in order to avoid infection. "That is wise dont you think Dad?" The patient had a tetanus shot, and the bandages had been removed from his scraped fingers. He was grateful, and lucky, that no bones had been shattered, and he expected to be back to Schio driving an ambulance in the mountains by the end of August. He told his family about the pictures he'd taken and the military souvenirs he'd scooped up—a dozen bayonets, helmets, knives, and much more.

The days and weeks after the birthday letter would bring surgeries and Hemingway's plaster-wrapped convalescence, which he turned into a Cognac-fueled social that lasted well past August, all the way to the armistice in November and into the winter. He

For his wounding while a Red Cross recruit in the war zone of the Piave River, Hemingway received Italy's War Merit Cross (left) as well as a Silver Medal of Military Valor. *Ernest Hemingway Collection, John F. Kennedy Presidential Library, Boston*

made friends with fellow patients, irritated the nursing leadership with his bad behavior, and fell in love with Agnes von Kurowsky, an American on the first international posting of a long career in Red Cross service. They were just crazy kids, she'd say much later. Yet their fling, and the emotional toll Hemingway suffered when she broke it off months later, took on epic proportions. A decade in the future, he'd reimagine those memories and the Italian wartime landscape in a resonant, provocative, and thoroughly modern novel.

14

LIES AND DISILLUSIONMENT

Ugly short infantry of the mind,
Advancing over difficult terrain.
—ERNEST HEMINGWAY, "MITRAILLIATRICE"

Grace Hall Hemingway chafed at her son's willful independence, as is evidenced in letters she wrote to him and in her
reaction to his real and imagined behaviors. Hemingway at times
tried to be honest and direct, and the war had certainly focused his
gaze and deepened his exchanges with his mother and father, even
as he omitted key details. His independent streak had led him to
a hospital bed in Milan. "I wouldn't say that it was hell," Hemingway wrote to his parents that year, "because that's been a bit overworked since General Sherman's time, but there have been about
eight times when I would have welcomed hell, just on a chance it
couldn't come to the phase of war I was experiencing."

In the night, as Hemingway struggled with sleep in his bed at
the Ospedale della Croce Rossa Americana in Milan, his mind
would go back in time. He tried to remember everything that
happened before he went to the war—or at least the wounded
Nick Adams in "Now I Lay Me" engaged in that mental exercise.

He traveled back to the woods and waters of Michigan. To the trout streams. To the house in Oak Park. To all the girls he knew. To scenes of his parents. To the moments before a shrapnel-filled mortar shell exploded three feet away from him.

Hemingway's wounding, his experience in the war, and what he learned there became the subject, openly or indirectly, of several of the short stories and novels he would write in the coming years. "His injury at Fossalta hardly provided the only key to unlock his writing and his personality," Scott Donaldson has written. "But he did abandon there his romantic concept of combat, to be replaced by a healthy disillusionment about war in general and World War I in particular." That disillusionment, sometimes acidic, often couched in humor, infuses nearly every page of *A Farewell to Arms*. It's the subtle, submerged subtext of the "lost generation" at the heart of *The Sun Also Rises*. It triggers the overt, excremental ritual that Colonel Cantwell performs on the banks of the Piave in *Across the River and into the Trees*, which finds Hemingway still reexamining his first war and his conflicted consciousness three decades after his extraordinary eighteenth year.

"When you go to war as a boy," Hemingway wrote in the 1940s, "you have a great illusion of immortality. Other people get killed; not you. . . . Then when you are badly wounded the first time you lose that illusion and you know it can happen to you. After being severely wounded two weeks before my nineteenth birthday I had a bad time until I figured out that nothing could happen to me that had not happened to all men before me. Whatever I had to do men had always done. If they had done it then I could do it too and the best thing was not to worry about it."

Hemingway had a way of projecting a sense of self-certainty, of hard-won knowledge, of possessing the truth of experience. He was the consummate expert, and often the consummate bullshitter. It served him well at the poker table, if you can believe his tales of bluffing and winning. He was the "braggart warrior," the *miles gloriosus*, as Donaldson determined, who told tall tales about himself in World War I and repeated similar, self-boosting yarns about his military activity in the Spanish Civil War and World War II. "He was hasty, impulsive—not to say impetuous," Agnes von Kurowsky Stanfield would say forty years after their hospital fling in Milan. "He didn't really know what he wanted. He hadn't clearly thought out anything." Yet even as his immaturity lingered, like so many wound stripes worn proudly on his sleeve, Hemingway's self-image took on a strain of gravity. Later that year, Hemingway told his family he'd stay in Italy until the war was over; he'd hobble for the Red Cross as long as he could. He reiterated the danger of the ambulance service. No one should worry, he wrote, "because it has been fairly conclusively proved that I cant be bumped off." Wounds were nothing, and he knew that from experience. "We all offer our bodies up and only a few are chosen, but it shouldn't reflect any special credit on those that are chosen." Hemingway was proud that his body had been chosen, yet he asserted that the dead are the real heroes, and so are the parents of the dead. To Hemingway, it was preferable "to die in all the happy period of undisillusioned youth, to go out in a blaze of light." That beats carrying on into old age with a tired body and shattered illusions. Hemingway's philosophizing prompted a need for acknowledgment: "Does all that sound like the crazy wild kid you sent out to learn about the world a year ago?"

As news filtered back to the states about Hemingway's wounding, his friends responded. Charles Hopkins sent a letter to Dr. Hemingway expressing "only feebly the sincere admiration I cherish for that husky son of yours; there isn't anything I can say that will add to the pride you must feel for that boy—he's a winner, that's all." Hopkins celebrated "Ernest's magnificent bravery, his conduct under fire, his fortitude in the face of wound and discomfort" and added, "Ernest certainly has had the chance of a life-time to prove his character, and I humbly ask as one of his friends to be permitted to share in the rejoicing over the manner in which he won his Cross." Tubby Williams wrote to Hemingway's parents of his "profound pride." Hemingway's valor was "no surprise to me" and "only typical of dear old 'Hemmy.'" Williams affirmed his great fondness for the young man from Oak Park and his promising talent: "He commanded more admiration from me tha[n] any young chap I had ever known to state in the romantic news paper game. I studied and loved him."

One day in late July, as Ernest lay in his hospital bed, a friendly postcard arrived. On the front side was a scene from Kansas City, a nighttime shot looking south along Main Street from the Junction, at Ninth Street. Two streetcars and motorcars clogging the road; rugged four- and five-story buildings lining the way, their windows illuminated; people walking the sidewalks that Hemingway walked not all that long ago. It might not have been home, but it must have registered as a place of friendship and comfort. The card had come from Ted Brumback's mother, Elizabeth Pratt Brumback. She'd read about Hemingway's wounding in the *Star*, a story prompted by a telegram from the Red Cross that made its way to Arabell Hemingway, his aunt, at 3629 Warwick Boulevard. ("Ernest Hemingway, in Italian ambulance service, temporary doing rolling canteen work, wounded; not dangerous," was the brief message as reported in the newspaper. Hemingway, the story added, was "the first casualty to any of *The Star*'s 132 former employees now fighting with the Allies.") "We are very proud of you here in K.C.," Mrs. Brumback wrote. She hoped Ernest would get well and join her "other boy" Ted, because he was surely lonesome without his Kansas City friend, "a lonesome Jonathan without his David."

For his part, Brumback entertained Hemingway with news from the Schio Country Club. And he had seen some of Hemingway's belongings, which were being held for him at Vicenza. "Your pants and shoe caused a great commotion, those for miles around coming in to see the curiosity," Brumback wrote two days before Hemingway's birthday, "and even Angelo decided that over two hundred perforations were no exaggeration. . . . You've certainly got some rep now Ernie, old boy, and if you come home with that medal—well x x x x."

Not long thereafter, Brumback learned that Hemingway's wounds were more serious than he had realized and had reported to the family in Oak Park. Brumback thought Hemingway would be back in Schio within a couple of weeks, but he heard from some section mates how they'd seen the young man "on a wheeling chair being triumphantly led thru the streets of Milan." Brumback reported to Hemingway that he had been running a canteen near Fornaci, Hemingway's original assignment near the front. It was convenient enough that he'd found Hemingway's sheepskin coat with which to ward off the early morning chill, since the practice was to visit the trenches at about 4:00 AM. "The rest of your stuff is all in Vicenza," Brumback wrote, and it was his intention to retrieve it and get it shipped to the hospital in Milan. Brumback's mother had told him that she'd visited the *Star*, where she spotted a bulletin board posting of the send-off story that included mug shots of both young men. Several "witty remarks" had been affixed to the posting, but Mrs. Brumback failed to record them.

Brumback and Hemingway corresponded often in the years after the war. Hemingway toyed with the idea of returning to newspaper work in Kansas City, but by 1920 Brumback suggested he wouldn't be able to make $200 a month, as he was looking for, and Pete Wellington might not be hiring anyway. Hemingway had dinner one night with Brumback in 1928, the year that the now-famous writer returned to Kansas City for the birth of his son, Patrick. The night didn't go well, according to a regret-filled letter in which Brumback apologized for his drunken behavior. Brumback later wrote to Hemingway a brief note of condolence after he'd learned of Clarence Hemingway's suicide. His own father, Judge Hermann Brumback, had gone the same way, so he could share Hemingway's grief with great understanding. By 1929 Brumback's marriage had decayed, and he moved to California to live with his mother. In the 1930s, Brumback returned to Kansas City and got back to the real estate business. He was living there when he offered the *Star* his colorful, though not always reliable, remembrance of Hemingway before the war.

As it turned out, Hemingway's path after the war took him to another *Star*, the newspaper in Toronto. He wrote in Toronto, and then filed stories from Europe. Six years after his November in Kansas City, Hemingway's mind traveled back there for a feature story about culinary adventures, his experience with "sea slugs, muskrat, porcupine, beaver tail . . . snails, eels, sparrows, caviar and spaghetti." Kansas City was "a great eating town," he wrote. It offered the comfort of all-night Mexican lunch wagons and the challenge of making his way through the lengthy menu of a Chinese restaurant near his first newspaper, "a real chop suey, chow mein place with teakwood tables and a fan-tan game going in the back room." He was still eighteen then, and he engaged in his "scientific gastronomic research" mostly by himself, because he couldn't get anyone to share some of the odd corners of the adventure. Especially the sea slugs, whose variations filled half a page of the seven-page menu. And the ancient eggs, which proved to be an instant turnoff. To his Toronto readers Hemingway revealed, in his yarning way, that he "was constantly in debt to various police sergeants, pugilists and wrestling promoters that winter." His dining experience wasn't cheap, he explained, and the Chinese restaurant owner, though grateful for Hemingway's loyalty, never extended him credit. "I think he was afraid I might die on him."

This piece also recounted the disputed story about the fistfight in a diner near the *Star* when Hemingway supposedly rose to protect the honor of Leo Fitzpatrick from a knife-wielding waiter, who'd misconstrued an order for milk toast. Curiously, Hemingway obscures who did what to whom and which reporter sent the waiter crashing into the glass cigar case. Instead of boasting about his fistic prowess, which was Hemingway's typical tactic, his obfuscation here adds to one's skepticism about his role in the incident and lends credence to Marcel Wallenstein's complaint that Hemingway wasn't even there.

Regardless, as his story went, the melee at the diner forced Hemingway and his newspaper friends to retreat to an all-night lunch wagon, which was the "glory" of Kansas City's "nocturnal life":

Many a night I have stood in the shelter of an all-night lunch wagon while the blizzard swept down from the great cold funnel of the Missouri River valley and eaten chili con carne, brown, red and hot all the way down, and real chilmaha frijoles while I learned about life and Mexican home cooking from the keeper of the wagon. To be invited inside an all-night lunch wagon was a great honor only accorded to the elect. The owners were all wonderful cooks, too.

Hemingway, of course, is calling attention here to his status as one of "the elect." Perhaps it was a perk of being a newspaper reporter, even one who was a sometimes awkward rookie. Still, there was one more benefit to the Mexican lunch wagon in Kansas City. One wagon's operator, he wrote, deserves credit for loaning Hemingway a copy of Stephen Crane's *The Red Badge of Courage*. Hemingway came to admire the book greatly, not least because Crane invented the story without having seen the war, a lesson he himself put to use when writing about the retreat at Caporetto in *A Farewell to Arms*. Years later, in the midst of World War II, Hemingway paid respect to Crane by reprinting the entire book in his anthology of great war writing, calling it "one of the finest books of our literature."

After the first war, and after he returned home from Italy, and after Agnes von Kurowsky broke his heart, Hemingway removed himself to upper Michigan for a while. It was at least in part an escape from the oppressiveness and unreasonable expectations of Oak Park. He bellied up to a typewriter and addressed the self-realization he had announced just a few months earlier, when he told his family that "the Lord ordained differently for me and I was made to be one of those beastly writing chaps y'know." He began writing short stories, but the magazines he sent them to were not interested. Kansas City was still on his mind. It was as yet unresolved whether he'd go back for another stint on the newspaper. But his days on the cops and crime beat came back to him easily as he crafted an odd story about a middling reporter who sets out to solve a murder case—the Punk Alford story. Later came a tough-guy tale about a contract killer named Hand (for Hand of God) Evans, a nemesis cop named Jack Farrell, and a booze-filled streetscape that melds Kansas City and Chicago.

"Jack Farrell" happened to be the name of a real Kansas City detective, whom Hemingway had written about at least once for the newspaper. It was Farrell who shot the cigar store robbers in November 1917, a Kansas City street crime story that Hemingway covered and a few years later, in Paris, transformed into one of his modernist vignettes. In "The Ash Heel's Tendon," Hemingway portrayed Farrell, the "czar of the Fifteenth Street police station," as a brilliant strategist who defeats Hand Evans with a dose of Enrico Caruso singing Pagliacci. The story was never published in Hemingway's lifetime.

Hemingway returned physically to Kansas City in later years, and at least two of those visits coincided with a work in progress. In 1928 he and his second wife, Pauline Pfeiffer Hemingway, were awaiting the birth of their son Patrick as Hemingway was nearing the end of *A Farewell to Arms*. Pauline's long, difficult labor and the resulting Caesarean delivery was an emotional experience that Hemingway could mine as he imagined the closing episode of his novel. Three years later, the couple returned for the birth of son Gregory. At the time, Hemingway was writing *Death in the Afternoon*, his exploration of bullfighting. Early on, the book includes a somewhat incongruous passage about Kansas City. In it, Hemingway time-travels to the city and connects two images that he experienced ten years apart. His memory links a blazing sunrise on the horizon in 1928 to a fire in the stockyards he covered for the paper. The memories come in the context of staying up late in Madrid and taking pleasure in seeing the sunrise in Constantinople. Close readers of Hemingway may consider a minor subtheme that leads to one of the more perplexing observations he ever made about the city—the opening lines of "God Rest You Merry, Gentlemen." In the story, which he wrote a few months after his 1931 return to Kansas City, Hemingway's journalist narrator visits with two ambulance surgeons on Christmas Day, when he hears about an oversexed teenager who'd come to the hospital wanting to be castrated. But before that story line develops, Hemingway begins with this: "In those days the distances were all very different, the dirt blew off the hills that now have been cut down, and

Kansas City was very like Constantinople. You may not believe this. No one believes this, but it is true."

The critic Harold Bloom didn't believe it and called the comparison outrageous. ("You can parody that by saying: 'In those days, Bridgeport, Connecticut, was very much like Haifa.'") Others have puzzled over it for years. Patrick Hemingway thinks the connection is explained in an unpublished fragment. "It's the wooden houses," he told me in April 2016, a detail gleaned from a manuscript paragraph about a view in the distance of the dusty hills and wooden houses of Stamboul. Hemingway, in Kansas City, lived for a while in a wood-frame house, and that seemed, to Patrick, to settle the matter. Another theory might connect Constantinople's infamous fleshpot district, the Galata, with the nighttime dens of iniquity that Hemingway learned about in Kansas City. Along with that, and perhaps the dust and stink he writes about Constantinople elsewhere, the sunrise seems to make the most sense. Hemingway says he never saw the sun come up in Madrid, because when it got too hot people waited until the coolest moments before sunrise to go to sleep. But in Constantinople and at least that one time in Kansas City, the fireball morning sun was memorable enough to make a psychic connection in a writer's creative wheelhouse. It was certainly good and believable enough for fiction.

––––––––––––

Hemingway began processing pieces of his war experience in fiction and poetry beginning in the summer of 1919, just a year after his wounding in Italy. In "The Passing of Pickles McCarty, or the 'Woppian Way,'" one of those early rejected stories, Hemingway imagined an Italian boxer who takes an Irish name and gives up the ring to fight with the Arditi, Italy's shock troops in the mountains. As biographer Jeffrey Meyers interprets it, "The autobiographical story portrays the tough Hemingway, stifled by Oak Park, who gives up journalism to join the Red Cross, wins a medal and is overwhelmed by banal conditions when he comes home." Meyers at least can be credited with calling the story "crudely crafted."

Hemingway also began reading extensively about the war, in magazines and books. Some of that likely reading, which Michael Reynolds detailed in *Hemingway's First War*, affirmed and rounded out the war that Hemingway had witnessed firsthand. Some of it gave him important accounts of other aspects of the war before he'd gotten there, including the retreat at Caporetto, which he'd only read about in the newspaper—it happened a week after his arrival in Kansas City. All of it, as Reynolds noted, served as fodder for *A Farewell to Arms*: "He was able to pick up second-hand stories, newspaper accounts, as well as histories and historical fiction, and use them all to his own purpose."

To Harold Krebs, Hemingway's protagonist in "Soldier's Home," "It was the most interesting reading he had ever done. . . . Now he was really learning about the war." Krebs is the shattered marine who has returned to Oklahoma from the war too late for adulation, sits on his porch reading histories, looks at the girls across the street with repressed longing, disappoints his mother with his lassitude and his distance, and thinks about going to Kansas City to get a job. Krebs "did not want to talk about the war." From June 1918 to the armistice, Krebs had seen action from Belleau Wood to the Argonne Forest in France. Now all he could do was to lie about it. No one would listen otherwise. As a result, he had developed a "distaste for everything that had happened to him in the war . . . because of the lies he had told."

When he sat down to write poems not long after the war, Hemingway picked through memories of his own and others.

There was one about "Roarin thru Schio town / Three days leave and a feelin free." Another, "Champs d'Honneur," surveys the dead and dying on a battlefield: "Soldiers pitch and cough and twitch; / All the world roars red and black, / Soldiers smother in a ditch / Choking through the whole attack." The "red and black" may well have reflected Hemingway's postwar awareness of *The Red and the Black*; Stendhal's other prominent novel, *The Charterhouse of Parma*, lent Hemingway a vivid example of taking readers deep into disastrous battle. Other poems mention places in Italy, and one puts the reader, along with its speaker, into the murk of the Basso Piave, where "Desire and / All the sweet pulsing aches . . . Are gone into the sullen dark." The poem's title orients the reader: "Killed Piave—July 8—1918." That, of course, was the date of Hemingway's wounding at Fossalta, and so we find him contemplating death and lost desire. Reynolds, however, explores an intriguing notion that Hemingway could have been thinking about the death of Lt. Edward McKey, his rolling canteen predecessor. In an earlier version of the poem, according to Reynolds, Hemingway had the date in the title as June 15, 1918, the beginning of the Austrian offensive along the Piave. It was also the day before McKey was killed instantly by an artillery shell explosion. Moreover, Reynolds suggests that McKey's life offers several parallels to that of Frederic Henry in *A Farewell to Arms*. Both were in Europe before the war, had volunteered to drive ambulances, and were fluent in Italian. Once again, whether encountering lies in reality or lies of poetry or novel writing, readers of Hemingway must wrestle with his constant and deliberate inventions. This is "a central point in Hemingway's art of fiction," Reynolds wrote. "He never allowed reality to interfere with his fiction, and in the early years he did not allow his personal experience to dictate to his work as an artist. When art and biography were at odds, he would change the remembered experience to fit the needs of his writing." In another poem, "Mitrailliatrice," Hemingway draws a line between writing and the fragment-spewing artillery shell implied by the title. At the typewriter, which "chatters in mechanical staccato," Hemingway conceived of himself, the writer in the making, as deploying the "Ugly short infantry of the mind, / Advancing over difficult terrain."

On Armistice Day, Hemingway, now nineteen and still in Italy, wrote to his parents and vowed that in the coming year he'd go to war again: "The war to make the world Safe for Ernie Hemingway and I plan to knock 'em for a loop and will be a busy man for several years." Within just a few years, Hemingway was certainly knocking the literary world for a loop. Early on came his series of modernist vignettes that he turned out in Paris in 1922 and 1923. They read like prose poems chiseled in the raw, hard world of "difficult terrain." A handful of them emerged from the war chest that was growing exponentially in Hemingway's imagination. He pieced together and altered moments from his own experience and the sound and substance of other people's voices to create tiny but compressed and explosive stories in six or eight or nine sentences each. In the composition of his book of stories they played like sharp-edged fragments, in one way like bursts of a teletype emitting a bulletin, in another like the cubist collages of Picasso and Braque, as Thomas Strychacz has suggested. In one vignette, for example, a British soldier recounts shooting Germans who were climbing over a garden wall at Mons, Belgium, site of the first western front battle of World War I. In one of the longest vignettes, "Nick"—probably a version of Nick Adams—sits wounded outside a church. Unlike Hemingway, he'd been shot in the spine. The bodies of Austrian soldiers lay nearby.

He's awaiting stretcher bearers and tries to speak to Rinaldi, who's lying against the wall. Nick tells him, "You and me we've made a separate peace." Hemingway later fleshed out remnants of his own war experience in three short stories set in Italy, in a post-war masterpiece of introspection and healing ("Big Two-Hearted River") and others. All of the war stories appeared alongside other pieces of short fiction that were inspired by his youth in Michigan and his reporting in Kansas City.

Then, before he turned thirty, Hemingway composed his symphonic treatment of the ambulance driver who makes a separate peace in *A Farewell to Arms*. That novel, following *In Our Time*, *The Sun Also Rises*, and the story collection *Men Without Women*, cemented Hemingway's reputation and insured that the life he had set out to make for himself at the age of eighteen, with all its emotional complications, human messiness, incessant braggadocio, and justifiable book-world acclaim, had come to fruition.

CODA

There was so much more about that year that Hemingway could dredge up when prompted. Eating oysters with Ernest Walsh at a fancy restaurant in Paris sent an odd sense memory through his brain. It reminded him of prostitutes in Kansas City back in his youthful stint there, and how they would finish up their task with the thought that swallowing the semen would serve as a curative, protecting them from "the con," if consumption was indeed what afflicted them. And Gertrude Stein and her dismissal of one of his Michigan stories as *inaccrochable*—essentially meaning unpublishable, because of its explicit sexual context—what did she know about sex? And besides, he was no naive sort and even knew a thing or two about homosexuality, given what he'd learned about tramps in the woods, and he was wary about the whole business, but the crime and hospital beat in Kansas City exposed him to so much in the way of *inaccrochable* matter. He could also tell tales about the Schio Country Club, his deepening friendships with Bill Horne and Ted Brumback in the shadow of the Dolomites, the poker games, and the convivial encounters with Italian townspeople in the bars. There very well could have been something close to *inaccrochable* going on there in the boredom before Hemingway found the real war at the front.

When the famous Hemingway, passing through Kansas City in 1940, told a *Star* reporter about that old police shootout he remembered covering, he didn't tell the whole story. He probably overstated his experience in one significant way and notably understated it in another.

January 5, 1918. Two Kansas City police detectives, Edward Kritser and Paul Conrad, were inside a house at 2743 Mercier Street, on the southwest edge of downtown. They were investigating drug dealers. When two other men approached the house, Conrad started shooting. The other men shot back. Turns out the second pair of men on the scene were not peddling drugs; they were federal revenue agents on the same mission as the detectives. John M. Tully and Albert Raithel were taken to General Hospital to treat their wounds. Tully was shot in the right leg, left arm, and abdomen. Raithel had wounds to his left wrist and midsection. Kritser and Conrad suffered little more than bullet holes in their clothes.

The case of mistaken identity among lawmen was not resolved until a backup police car, sent from the Nineteenth Street station, arrived at the house on Mercier. The revolver battle occurred late on a Saturday afternoon, just in time for a truncated news story to appear in the last edition of that day's *Star*. Hemingway, probably working with other reporters, spent the next several hours fleshing out the story for the Sunday edition. The reporters gained conflicting accounts of the incident from Tully on the one side and Kritser and Conrad on the other. Raithel was hospitalized and inaccessible that night. In addition, according to the story, the US district attorney, Francis M. Wilson, conferred that night with the police chief and suggested there might be a backstory to the gun battle with details he wouldn't disclose.

In his interview with Paul Fisher in 1940, Hemingway left the impression that he had been present as the revolvers flashed and bullets hailed from one side of the street to the other. As Fisher wrote, Hemingway "lay under a Ford while detectives shot two internal revenue agents." Reading the news stories from that winter day in 1918 and later, as well as witness testimony contained in the federal case files, could lead one to the conclusion that Hemingway, once again, was inflating his involvement in a wild-side event. It is quite possible that Hemingway motored over with the backup police car and thus caught the very end of the fracas, perhaps even rolling under a Ford as the last shots were fired before someone yelled, "They're government men." But that seems like a long shot. Hemingway clipped the Sunday story, headlined BATTLE OF RAID SQUADS and running more than an entire column on the front page, and mailed it back home. In a letter dated January 8, he bragged to his sister Marcelline about his big, roaring scoop and how he "nearly got bumped off" in the process. But he warned her not to share the letter, just the clipping, leaving his brush with danger—or yet another tall tale—just between them.

Hemingway's involvement in the gun-battle story extended beyond his contribution to the reporting on Saturday, January 5. Four days before he left Kansas City, his apprenticeship over and the ambulance service on the horizon, a federal grand jury indicted the two city detectives, Kritser and Conrad, for interfering with the federal agents and shooting them. Thirty witnesses had appeared before the grand jury, according to the *Star* on April 26, 1918. What the story did not report, and what Hemingway never apparently told anyone—not his family and not Paul Fisher of the *Star* in November 1940—was that one of those witnesses was Hemingway himself.

Years ago, biographer Mike Reynolds told me of his suspicion that Hemingway had testified before a grand jury while in Kansas City. And over the years I tried numerous times to confirm that. I'd long assumed that a state court grand jury would have involved Hemingway's coverage of the alleged graft and mismanagement of the city hospitals. The grand jury records of the Jackson County

Circuit Court from 1918 eluded me, and I could find no coverage by the newspaper of a grand jury investigation into the hospital problems. Then it occurred to me only recently, as I was completing this book, that I'd gone down the wrong path. When I found the federal court case of the US government versus Edward C. Kritser and Paul O. Conrad, the documents miraculously contained the evidence that confirmed Reynolds's hunch.

The files of case No. 3541 were neatly folded, stacked, and wrapped by a dark fuchsia ribbon. An archivist at the National Archives Regional Center in Kansas City had found the files within minutes of my arrival. As I pored over the documents in the quiet research room, I could take a measure of the slow drip of justice as the case dragged out for months. It was well into 1919 before a trial was scheduled. But soon came the indictment document itself, which laid out six counts against Kritser and Conrad. As I folded the thick document back up, I noticed more information on the back of the last page. It was a list of names headed WITNESSES. And there, a little more than halfway down the list, was typed E.M. HEMINGWAY. Ernest Miller Hemingway. The name of W. B. Moorhead, the *Star*'s principal police reporter, sometimes known as "Broken Bill," was also on the list. The evidence undercuts Moorhead's suggestion years later that Hemingway would have had nothing to do with the "battle of the raid squads" story. Matthew Bruccoli mentioned Moorhead's notion, based on information and opinion from another *Star* writer in the 1960s, in his compilation of *Star* stories, *Ernest Hemingway, Cub Reporter*. Bruccoli did not believe Moorhead either.

Although the *Star* story on April 26 about the indictment noted there'd been thirty witnesses, this list added up to thirty-two. So perhaps the evidence raises more questions than it answers. Did Hemingway and Moorhead really testify? Did the *Star* fiddle with the number or omit details from all the stories to hide both

Witnesses:
John M. Rodgers
John M. Tully
Nettie Lenhart
Mary Stewart (col)
Chief Thomas B. Flahiv
Harry L. Arnold
Albert Raithel
John H. Virgin
John B. Nester
Carrie M. Nester
John L. Ghent
Mary Alice Fuqua
Michael A. Cassidy
Don Martin
Mrs. Rose Stanton
Dr. Allen Porter
R. Emery
Doll G. Pigg
Grace Vega
E. M. Hemingway
Sallie Benton (col)
Corinne Stewart (col)
W. B. Moorhead
Ida Davis
H. R. Blevins
James A. Savage
Anthony P. Fonda
Dwight E. Gillson
W. J. Cassiday
Maggie Rhone (col)
Arthur T. Bagley
Richard Carl Adams

A federal grand jury indictment on April 26, 1918, followed testimony by thirty-two witnesses, according to one document, including Ernest Hemingway. Four witnesses were identified as "(col)," or "colored." *National Archives at Kansas City, Missouri*

Hemingway's role as an on-the-street witness and the rare event that a newspaperman would have testified before a grand jury?

As it happens, a county grand jury also met in March, and in early April 1918 prosecutors announced an indictment of two dozen laundry strikers and rioters. This was a story Hemingway also knew quite well, and given his role as an acknowledged witness of rock throwing in one of those incidents, it wouldn't surprise me if long-sealed documents could be turned up in the state court archives that showed the eighteen-year-old reporter—and perhaps Moorhead as well—testified before still another grand jury.

Just when it seemed there was nothing new to be learned about the most examined American writer of the twentieth century.

ACKNOWLEDGMENTS

In researching the life and work of Ernest Hemingway, all roads lead to the John F. Kennedy Presidential Library and Museum. Overlooking Boston Harbor, I. M. Pei's bright white building holds the vast Ernest Hemingway Collection of manuscripts, correspondence, photographs, artworks, and memorabilia. It's an essential starting point, or at least it was for me when I began my journey into Hemingway, a relative latecomer, in 1999, the one-hundredth anniversary of his birth. I am grateful for what I found there and for the help and guidance I received from its staffers over the years, including Stephen Plotkin, Susan Wrynn, James Hill, Maryrose Grossman, Connor Anderson, and others.

It was in the Hemingway Collection at the JFK, for example, that I experienced an emotional moment of discovery more than ten years ago. Reading one of T. Norman Williams's letters gave me a revelation about Hemingway's emerging talent that seemed unprecedented in the testimony of his contemporaries at the Kansas City newspaper in 1917–18 (see chapter 12). It also gave me a lump in my throat. At the time I was wobbling between naïveté and despair over the prospect of developing this inquiry into Hemingway's early influences. As any researcher knows, the process of leafing through folders and ancient correspondence can be slow, frustrating, occasionally enlightening, often invigorating. The voice of Tubby Williams gave me new inspiration and confidence that there was still a story to tell about Hemingway's early life.

I am also grateful for the moments of personal connection that the Hemingway Collection and the Kennedy Library prompted, including the chance to chat during that first visit with Carol Hemingway Gardner, Ernest's youngest sister and at the time his last living sibling. My annual visits to the Kennedy Library for the PEN/Hemingway Award events have frequently included jolly meetings with Patrick Hemingway and his wife, Carol; grandson Seán Hemingway and his family; and other Hemingway descendants.

Research and special collection staffs at the Newberry Library in Chicago, the Oak Park Public Library, the Ernest Hemingway Foundation of Oak Park, New York Public Library, the Firestone Library at Princeton University, University of Delaware Library, the Library of Congress, the Harry Ransom Center at the University of Texas, the Beinecke Library at Yale University, the Lilly Library at Indiana University, and Missouri Valley Special Collections at the Kansas City Public Library were always accessible and helpful, and I'm grateful for the permission they granted for using various materials.

Two leading Hemingway scholars, my friends Susan Beegel and Scott Donaldson, were early readers of early pieces of the book. Their criticisms and enthusiasm were valuable and gave me courage to continue. Other members of the Ernest Hemingway Society and Foundation gave welcome guidance and encouragement, including Kirk Curnutt, Linda Patterson Miller, Sandy Spanier, H. R. Stoneback, Miriam Mandel, Valerie Hemingway, Linda Wagner-Martin, and Alex Vernon. Gail Sinclair and Steven Trout, my *War + Ink* coeditors and conference co-coordinators, were a solid and supportive team buttressing the study of the early Hemingway years. Along with Susan Beegel, the longtime editor of the *Hemingway Review*, the late Paul Montgomery was as responsible as anyone for my enlistment in Hemingway studies. As a retired *New York Times* reporter, Montgomery invited me, a fellow journalist, not an academic, into the inner sanctum of the Hemingway Society, giving me a place at a conference table to deliver a paper in 2002 at Stresa, Italy.

Thanks also to other early readers, whose feedback can be found in these pages: Malka Margolies, Justin Martin, Greg Michalson, Amanda Vaill, Candice Millard, and Paul Hendrickson, who generously contributed the foreword. Pep talks with Steve Weinberg, Tom Shawver, Brian Shawver, Whitney Terrell, Michelle Boisseau, Tom Stroik, Richard Serrano, Gaylord Torrence, Marjorie Alexander, Richard and Ginger Rhodes, Tim O'Brien, Donna Seaman, and other writing friends kept my energy going.

Thanks to Brian Burnes, Cruise Palmer, and my friend, the late Jim McKinley, for sharing Hemingway and *Star* material from their files. Credit also to Mark Zieman, a former editor and publisher at the *Kansas City Star* (now an executive at McClatchy), whose Hemingway studies predated mine and led to the creation of a Hemingway website, some of which remains accessible. As longtime librarian and custodian of records at the *Star*, Derek Donovan was extremely helpful over the years.

Ernie Mainland, Hemingway's nephew, graciously spent time showing us Windemere cottage and Walloon Lake, and, long before they were published, gave me copies of pertinent letters, including the one from April 16, 1918, which I consider the most important letter Hemingway wrote home from Kansas City.

Stephen L. Harris, who plowed the ground of early twentieth-century *Kansas City Star* history forty years ago, graciously shared his voluminous correspondence files, other documents, and his unpublished manuscript.

Ann Reynolds was kind enough to let me inspect her late husband Michael's files in their Santa Fe home. Charles A. Fenton Jr. and Paul Quintanilla granted me permission to use material from their fathers's works. And the late John Sanford, Hemingway's nephew and son of Marcelline Hemingway Sanford, allowed me to quote from his mother's book. Harry Haskell granted permission to quote from Henry Haskell's letters to Fenton.

At Chicago Review Press, Lisa Reardon believed in the book from the get-go. Ellen Hornor and Michelle Williams performed impressive acts of eagle-eye editing and saved me from numerous gaffes.

And lastly, nothing but thanks and love to my longtime companion, Carol Zastoupil. She didn't sign up to become a Hemingway tourist, but in our travels over the years her patience and good humor and sincere interest were priceless. As was her understanding as I disappeared behind my books and laptop screen.

APPENDIX

Three stories from Ernest Hemingway's Kansas City apprenticeship are reproduced here with permission.

"Kerensky, the Fighting Flea"

This story, most likely Hemingway's first extended feature article for the newspaper, appeared in the Kansas City Star *on December 16, 1917.*

Somehow, although he is the smallest office boy around the place, none of the other lads pick on him. Scuffling and fighting almost has ceased since Kerensky came to work. That's only one of the nicknames of Leo Kobreen, and was assigned to him because of a considerable facial resemblance to the perpetually fleeing Russian statesman, and, too, because both wore quite formal standing collars.

In size, Leo is about right for spanking. But that never will happen to Leo. Although he is inches short of five feet, there is a bulkiness about his shoulders that gains respect even from those Cossacks of the business world, the messenger boys.

In fact, it was a messenger, coming in blusteringly, who first made it known that Leo possessed a reputation. Almost politely the cocky young fellow handed a yellow envelope to the office bantam.

"Why it's Kid Williams," he said, "Are you going to fight at the club Saturday night, Kid?"

"I should have known it," the boss said, "Kerensky has all the characteristics of a prize fighter. After a short round of work doesn't he retire to a corner and sit down?"

Then some of them remembered Kid Williams in preliminary bouts. One of those boys who scrap three rounds before the big fighters enter the ring. That's Kerensky.

You may have thrown some loose change into the ring at the final gong. How you laughed to see the two bantams push each other about and scramble fiercely each to pick up the most. Sometimes they couldn't wait to get their gloves off. All the fight fans roared at them trying to pick up thin dimes in their padded fists.

"That's all hippodrome stuff," Kerensky says. "The men like to see us quarrel over the money, but win or lose, we split it fifty-fifty. My half of the pickup runs from $1.50 to $2.50."

The worst thing about the fight game, take it from Kerensky, is the smoke. He has even considered retiring from the ring because it is so upsetting to take a deep breath of tobacco fumes.

"But of course I haven't quit," he explains. "Right now if I knew some of the clubs downtown had a smoker on and they offered me $2, of course I'd get in and fight."

How would Kerensky advise a young man to open a pugilistic career? Well, he just picked up his skill. For several years he sold papers, and you know how one thing leads to another. There is a newsboy rule that if one boy installs himself on a corner no other can sell there. A full grown man used to cry the headlines on a certain Grand Avenue crossing. Poachers bothered him.

"It wouldn't look right for a big fellow to hit a little kid," says Kerensky, "so he let me sell there, too, and sicked me on all the strange boys. I always ran them away. He liked me and called me Kid Williams, after the bantamweight champion."

Kerensky's last street fight was to a big gate. A newsboy of larger growth was the victim. They clinched and fell to the sidewalk. A crowd gathered, but the crossing patrolman turned his back till the battle was over. Then he came over and said: "Leo, I guess you'll have to cut this out."

After that, when Leo wanted to fight, somebody had to hire a hall. He began going into the gymnasiums to sell papers. There he watched the big men train for their Convention Hall bouts. Sometimes the proprietors would let him come in and work out beside Thorpe or Chavez for nothing. It costs the ordinary citizen a dime, Leo says, to get in and work at the pulleys and weights at times like these.

His opportunity came to go on in a newsboy bout at a smoker in Cutler's gymnasium. The kid glows yet at the mention of that bout.

"It was the best fight of my career," he says. "I went in mad, and gave the fans their money's worth. But I was awful green, and was almost knocked out in the last round. Now I know how to study 'em, and I don't have to work as hard."

After hard days in old Russia, the life is full of joy for Leo, and who can say that he is not making the most of his opportunities? When he talks of the past it is of a pogram [*sic*]. That Christmas season the workmen in a sugar refinery near Kiev made a cross of ice and set it up on the frozen river. It fell over and they blamed the Jews. Then the workmen rioted, breaking into stores and smashing windows. Leo and his family hid on the roof for three days, and his sister fell ill of pneumonia. One studies to change the subject and asks:

"Leo, do they ever match you with a bigger boy?"

"Oh no," he says, "the crowd wouldn't stand for that. But sometimes I catch one on the street."

"At the End of the Ambulance Run"

First published in the Kansas City Star *on January 20, 1918.*

The night ambulance attendants shuffled down the long, dark corridors at the General Hospital with an inert burden on the stretcher. They turned in at the receiving ward and lifted the unconscious man to the operating table. His hands were calloused and he was unkempt and ragged, a victim of a street brawl near the city market. No one knew who he was, but a receipt, bearing the name of George Anderson, for $10 paid on a home out in a little Nebraska town served to identify him.

The surgeon opened the swollen eyelids. The eyes were turned to the left. "A fracture on the left side of the skull," he said to the attendants who stood about the table. "Well, George, you're not going to finish paying for that home of yours."

"George" merely lifted a hand as though groping for something. Attendants hurriedly caught hold of him to keep him from rolling from the table. But he scratched his face in a tired, resigned way that seemed almost ridiculous, and placed his hand again at his side. Four hours later he died.

It was merely one of the many cases that come to the city dispensary from night to night—and from day to day for that matter; but the night shift, perhaps, has a wider range of the life and death tragedy—and even comedy, of the city. When "George" comes in on the soiled, bloody stretcher and the rags are stripped off and his naked, broken body lies on the white table in the glare of the surgeon's light, and he dangles on a little thread of life, while the physicians struggle grimly, it is all in the night's work, whether the thread snaps or whether it holds so that George can fight on and work and play.

Here comes another case. This time a small man limps in, supported by an ambulance man and a big policeman in uniform. "Yes, sir, we got a real robber this time—a real one—just look at him!" the big officer smiled. "He tried to hold up a drug store, and the clerks slipped one over on him. It was a—"

"Yes, but they was three of 'em, an' they was shootin' all at once," the prisoner explained. Since there was no use in attempting to deny the attempted robbery, he felt justified in offering an alibi for his frustrated prowess.

"It looks like I oughtta got one of 'em, but then, maybe, I'll do better next time.

"Say, you'd better hurry up and get these clothes off of me, before they get all bloody. I don't want 'em spoiled." He was thoroughly defeated and dejected, and the red handkerchief he used for a mask still hung from his neck.

He rolled a cigarette, and as the attendants removed his clothes, a ball of lead rattled to the floor. "Whee! It went clear through, didn't it? Say, I'll be out before long, won't I, doc?"

"Yes—out of the hospital," the physician replied significantly.

Out on Twenty-seventh street a drug clerk—the one of the three who used the .38—has a .38 bullet dangling from his watch chain.

———————

One night they brought in a negro who had been cut with a razor. It is not a mere joke about negroes using the razor—they really do it. The lower end of the man's heart had been cut away and there was not much hope for him.

Surgeons informed his relatives of the one chance that remained, and it was a very slim one. They took some stitches in his heart and the next day he had improved sufficiently to be seen by a police sergeant.

"It was just a friend of mine, boss," the negro replied weakly to questioning. The sergeant threatened and cajoled, but the negro would not tell who cut him.

"Well, just stay there and die, then," the officer turned away exasperated.

But the negro did not die. He was out in a few weeks, and the police finally learned who his assailant was. He was found dead—his vitals opened by a razor.

"It's razor wounds in the African belt and slugging in the wet block. In Little Italy they prefer the sawed-off shotgun. We can almost tell what part of the city a man is from just by seeing how they did him up," one of the hospital attendants commented.

But it is not all violence and sudden death that comes to the attention of the emergency physicians. They attend the injuries and ills of charity patients. Here is a laborer who burned his foot one morning when he used too much kerosene in building the fire, and over there is a small boy brought in by his mother, who explains there is something the matter with his nose. An instrument is inserted into the nostril of the squirming youngster and is drawn forth. A grain of corn, just sprouted, dangles at the end of the steel.

One day an aged printer, his hand swollen from blood poisoning, came in. Lead from the type metal had entered a small scratch. The surgeon told him they would have to amputate his left thumb.

"Why, doc? You don't mean it do you? Why, that'd be worsen sawing the periscope off of a submarine! I've just gotta have that thumb. I'm an old-time swift. I could set my six galleys a day in my time—that was before the linotypes came in. Even now, they need my business, for some of the finest work is done by hand. And you go and take that finger away from me and—well, it'd be mighty interesting to know how I'd ever hold a 'stick' in my hand again. Why, doc!—"

With face drawn, and head bowed, he limped out the doorway. The French artist who vowed to commit suicide if he lost his right hand in battle might have understood the struggle the old man had alone in the darkness. Later that night the printer returned. He was very drunk.

"Just take the damn works, doc, take the whole damn works," he wept.

At one time a man from out in Kansas, a fairly likable and respectable sort of man to look at him, went on a little debauch when he came to Kansas City. It was just a little incident that the folks in the home town would never learn about. The ambulance brought him from a wine room, dead from a stroke of heart disease. At another time (it happens quite often) a young girl took poison. The physicians who saved her life seldom speak of the case. If she had died her story might have been told—but she has to live.

And so the work goes on. For one man it means a clean bed and prescriptions with whisky in it, possibly, and for another, it is a place in the potters' field. The skill of the surgeon is exercised just the same, no matter what the cause of the injury or the deserts of the patient.

The telephone bell is ringing again. "Yes, this is the receiving ward," says the desk attendant. "No. 4 Police Station, you say? A shooting scrape? All right they'll be right over." And the big car speeds down the Cherry Street hill, the headlights boring a yellow funnel into the darkness.

"Would 'Treat 'Em Rough'"

First published in the Kansas City Star *on April 18, 1918.*

Four men stood outside the army recruiting office at Twelfth Street and Grand Avenue at 7:45 o'clock this morning when the sergeant opened up. A stout, red faced man wearing a khaki shirt was the first up the stairs.

"I'm the treat 'em rough man," he bawled. "That cat in the poster has nothing on me. Where do you join the tankers?"

"Have to wait for Lieutenant Cooter," said the sergeant. "He decides whether you'll treat 'em rough or not."

The fat man waited outside the door. By 9 o'clock thirty men crowded the third floor hallway. The stout man was nearest the door. Just behind him was a gray haired man wearing a derby, a well cut gray suit, a purple tie, socks to match and a silk hand-kerchief with a light purple border peeping from his vest pocket.

"I'm over draft age and it doesn't matter what my profession is," he said. "I never really wanted to get into this war before, but the tanks are different. I guess I can treat 'em rough."

The crowd grew steadily. By 10 o'clock there were forty applicants. Some of the men were humming, others talking among themselves. The stout man, perspiration pouring down his face, held his place next the door. He tried to whistle, but his lips wouldn't pucker. He stood on one foot, then the other. He mopped his face with a handkerchief, and finally bolted out through the crowd.

"He looked pretty hot but he got cold feet," a mechanic in overalls commented.

After the fat man left there was a slight exodus. A high school boy with a geometry book decided in favor of school. Two flashily dressed youths said, "Aw, let's get a beer." One man, saying nothing, slipped away.

"Can't stand the gaff," said the mechanic.

But most of the applicants stayed. A youth wearing an army shirt explained: "It's my girl. I belonged to the home guards and she kind of kidded me. Nobody's going to kid a tanker, I guess."

The opinion of most of the men was voiced by a clerk.

"I don't know anything about tractors or machinery, but I can learn to work a machine gun and I want to get across. Gee, I hope I get in."

A little man with double lens glasses said: "I don't suppose they'll take me. Guess I'm pretty useless. But I want to try. It's about my last chance. They all throw me down."

When Lieut. Frank E. Cooter, special tank recruiting officer, appeared, the crowd formed a line outside the door. The men were admitted one at a time. Moistening their lips, they entered the little room and stated their qualifications.

John R. Ecklund, 27 years old, was one of the first admitted.

"What mechanical experience have you had?" he was asked.

"None. I'm an attorney for the Kansas City Street Railways Company," he replied.

"Why do you want to join?"

"I want to see action and get over in a hurry."

Lieutenant Cooter accepted him.

"That is the type of all of them," the lieutenant said. "That is what brings men here. Not promises of high pay or easy service, but telling the truth about quick action and danger. 'To know and yet to dare,' would be a good slogan. Quick service, quick promotion and action, action, is what brings them. They are the finest type of men for soldiers."

Besides Ecklund six other men were accepted for service up to noon.

NOTES

Prologue

front-page news: "Back to His First Field," *Kansas City Times*, November 26, 1940, 1.

"biggest beds": *Across the River and into the Trees*, 241.

"He still is the great chronicler": William M. Reddig, "The Bell Tolls for Thee," *Kansas City Star*, October 26, 1940, 16.

"awfully easy to be hard-boiled": *The Sun Also Rises*, 42.

"modest, rather shy": J. Charles "Carl" Edgar to Charles A. Fenton, April 13, 1952, Beinecke Rare Book and Manuscript Library, Yale University (hereafter cited as Beinecke).

"Cambiamos": An account of this meeting appears in Paul Quintanilla, "Don Quixote in the Heartland: My Father's Murals," *New Letters* 7, nos. 3 and 4 (2004): 104–5.

At least one Star *man*: Theodore M. O'Leary, interview with author, 1998.

Chapter 1: Summer of Indecision

so went the rumors: Wilhelmina Corlett to Charles A. Fenton, June 10, 1952, Beinecke.

detailed diaries: Numerous early documents are reproduced in Elder, Vetch, and Cirino, eds., *Hidden Hemingway*.

"citizens took pride": Nagel, "The Hemingways and Oak Park, Illinois: Background and Legacy," in Nagel, ed., *Ernest Hemingway*, 10.

"very arbitrary": J. Charles Edgar to Charles A Fenton, March 26, 1952, Beinecke.

"mother had little tolerance": Carol Hemingway Gardner, "Recollections," *The Hemingway Review* 24, no. 1 (Fall 2004): 23.

"Please don't burn": Hemingway to his mother, Spanier and Trogdon, eds., *Letters*, 40.

"Odgar always": "On Writing," *Nick Adams Stories*, 235.

"seek his fortune": Edgar to Fenton, March 26, 1952, Beinecke.

"nicer to Nick": "Summer People," in *Complete Short Stories*, 496.

"ingenuous a youth": Edgar to Fenton, March 26, 1952, Beinecke.

"1 worn out suit": Megan Desnoyers, "Ernest Hemingway: A Storyteller's Legacy," online: www.jfklibrary.org/Research/The-Ernest-Hemingway -Collection/Online-Resources/Storytellers-Legacy.aspx?p=2.

White told Hemingway: Baker, *A Life Story*, 30–31.

Hemingstein: Sanford, *At the Hemingways*, 128.

"After three years": Richard Harding Davis, "The Reporter Who Made Himself King," unpaginated, online: http://onlinebooks.library.upenn .edu/webbin/gutbook/lookup?num=407.

a brawl: Hemingway to Fannie Biggs, Spanier and Trogdon, *Letters*, 38–39.

"headstrong and abusive": Clarence Hemingway to Grace Hemingway, August 12, 1917, Harry Ransom Center, University of Texas, Austin.

"Brother Tyler": Ibid.

"in great shape": Hemingway to his father, Spanier and Trogdon, *Letters*, 52.

"Robert Jordan had not": *For Whom the Bell Tolls*, 405.

"Got any dope": *Nick Adams Stories*, 133–4.

"Mark Twain, Huck Finn": Ibid.

Marcelline believed: Sanford, *At the Hemingways*, 156.

"Oh Oinest": Lucille Dick to Hemingway, October 3, 1917, Ernest Hemingway Collection, John F. Kennedy Presidential Library and Museum, Boston (hereafter cited as EH Collection).

Chapter 2: Creative Cauldron

"all kinds of readers": E. B. Garnett, "The Editor-Builder Who Molded a City," *Kansas City Star*, special 85th anniversary edition, April 11, 1965.

"most dominant factor": Garnett, *Life on The Star*.

"stormy, dominating": quoted in Garnett, "The Editor-Builder."

"Nelson despised": Garnett, *Life on The Star*.

"Always keep in mind": members of the *Kansas City Star* staff, *William Rockhill Nelson: The Story of a Man and a Newspaper and a City* (Cambridge: Riverside, 1915), 118.

"your family were marooned": Garnett, *Life on The Star.*

"imbued with Nelson's ideals": Ibid.

"You are worth": Sumner Blossom to Stephen L. Harris, February 28, 1975. Private collection.

"no patience": Marvin Creager to Fenton, February 15, 1952, Beinecke.

If a reporter: Ibid.

journalism schools: Garnett, *Life on The Star.*

"Originality counted": Garnett to Fenton, February 26, 1952, Beinecke.

action in Italy: "Doctor Jenkins to Write of the Italian Campaign," *Kansas City Star*, October 15, 1917, 1.

"evil influences": "Vice Is a Big War Peril," *Kansas City Star*, October 15, 1917, 1.

downtown hotel rooms: "Christians to Flock Here," *Kansas City Star*, October 15, 1917, 3.

"alarums of war": Creager to Fenton, February 26, 1952, Beinecke.

"more life": Russel Crouse to Fenton, February 8, 1952, Beinecke.

"Use short sentences": "The Star Copy Style," online, downloadable PDF reproduction: www.kansascity.com/entertainment/books/article1063 2713.ece/BINARY/The%20Star%20Copy%20Style.pdf.

"full of don'ts": Creager to Fenton, February 15, 1952, Beinecke.

"both barrels": Ibid.

"His arms and legs": Dale Wilson to *Kansas City Star*, 1967. Wilson had been corresponding with biographer Carlos Baker and sent a reminiscence to the newspaper along with a copy of a letter Hemingway had sent him in May 1918.

"world's baseball series": "Soldiers Liked Scoreboard," *Kansas City Star*, October 17, 1917, 2.

"Lean Greyhounds": *Kansas City Star*, October 17, 1917, 18.

training in France: Ibid., 10.

Champagne and environs: Burris A. Jenkins, "In a Land of Camouflage," *Kansas City Star*, October 17, 8. Revised and reprinted in Jenkins, *Facing the Hindenburg Line*, 123–30. I first explored Jenkins's dispatches and their possible influence on Hemingway in somewhat different form in "Preparing for War and Writing: What the Young

Hemingway Read in *The Kansas City Star*, 1917–1918," *The Hemingway Review* 23, no. 2 (Spring 2004): 5–20.

"They will go grimly": Burris A. Jenkins, "Cupid Outranks Mars in Pershing's Army," *Kansas City Star*, October 15, 1917, 1 (Want Ad Section).

"vital importance": Theodore Roosevelt, "Broomstick Apologists," *Kansas City Star*, October 14, 1917, 1.

"Today I had 3 stories": Hemingway to family, Spanier and Trogdon, *Letters*, 53–54.

"his Harvard and his Yale": Baker, *The Writer as Artist*, 3.

Chapter 3: "The Morally Strenuous Life"

"vain, pompous man": Edgar to Fenton, March 26, 1952, Beinecke.

"No life is complete": Alfred T. Hemingway, *How to Make Good*.

a good-humored man: "Tyler Hemingway," *Kansas City Star*, February 27, 1922, 18.

"Everybody at the Star": Hemingway to his father, Spanier and Trogdon, *Letters*, 55

Sophie West: "Brought Girl from New York," *Kansas City Star*, October 23, 1917, 6.

"remarkably intense": Garwood, *Crossroads of America*, 321.

"who was run down": "Little Hope for Chief Vaughn," *Kansas City Star*, October 25, 1917, 1.

"a fighting man": "Speaking the Public Mind," *Kansas City Star*, February 1, 1918, 6.

"Belief and enthusiasm": Theodore Roosevelt, *American Ideals* (New York: G. P. Putnam, 1901), 53; quoted in Reynolds, *Young Hemingway*, 61.

"courage, love, honor": Reynolds, *Young Hemingway*, 163.

"Let him, if a man": Theodore Roosevelt, *The Foes of Our Own Household* (New York: Doran, 1917); quoted in Reynolds, *Young Hemingway*, 23. Online: www.theodore-roosevelt.com/images/research/foesofourownhousehold.pdf.

"regret with bitter shame": Theodore Roosevelt, "The Peace of Complete Victory," *Kansas City Times*, October 23, 1917, 1.

"make the cripple": Theodore Roosevelt, "The Passing of the Cripple," *Kansas City Star*, October 23, 1917, 1.

"they knew they had accomplished something": "And After the Celebration," *Kansas City Times*, October 25, 1917, 10.

"Speckled Robert": "The Umpire," *Kansas City Star*, October 23, 1917, 10.

"The death of Bob Fitzsimmons": Ibid.

Mrs. Ralph Wildbauhm: "Cop Found Her Bond Money," *Kansas City Times*, October 25, 1917, 12.

"Starbeams" quip: *Kansas City Star*, October 22, 1917, 14.

Lucie Lacoste: "Home Is Not a Prison," *Kansas City Star*, October 22, 1917, 9.

It praised Henry Allen: "A Great Reporter," *Kansas City Star*, October 24, 1917, 18.

"jazz forth": Hemingway to his sister, Spanier and Trogdon, *Letters*, 56.

"mere pittance": Ibid.

Chapter 4: "The Insignificance of Self"

"Those who talk": "Transports Our War Job," *Kansas City Star*, October 25, 1917, 1.

"This morning Lord Northcliffe": Hemingway to his father, Spanier and Trogdon, *Letters*, 54.

"I saw the only way": "Calls It a 'Long, Hard War,'" *Kansas City Star*, October 25, 1917, 1.

"Everybody that knows Italy": Burris Jenkins, "Italian Front a Keystone," *Kansas City Star*, October 24, 1917, 6.

"The Alps": Ibid.

"I remained equally convinced": Jenkins, *Where My Caravan Has Rested* (Chicago: Willett Clark, 1939), 89.

"northern wing": "Second Italian Army Retreating," *Kansas City Star*, October 26, 1917, 1.

"further evidence": "London Confident of Italy," *Kansas City Star*, October 26, 1917, 1.

"Blue fire flashes": "Angel of the Marne Here," *Kansas City Star*, October 19, 1917, 10B. A version of this section about the Countess Mazzuchi first appeared in Steve Paul, "Preparing for War and Writing: What the Young Hemingway Read in *The Kansas City Star*, 1917–1918," *The Hemingway Review* 23, no. 2 (Spring 2004): 5–20.

"Although the procession": "Crowds Enjoyed It All," *Kansas City Times*, October 25, 1917, 10.

"*It was a jolly crowd*": "And After the Celebration," *Kansas City Times*, October 25, 1917, 10.

As obituary writer: "He Did His Bit—Then Died," *Kansas City Times*, October 25, 1917, 10.

"*Believe me*": Spanier and Trogdon, *Letters*, 59.

"*One is overpowered*": Burris Jenkins, "Italian Front a Keystone," *Kansas City Star*, October 24, 1917, 6.

"*If they see*": *Complete Short Stories*, 308.

"*untold millions*": Ibid., 312.

"*That night we lay*": Ibid., 276.

"*the mulberry trees*": "Italy, a Country of Song," *Kansas City Star*, October 25, 1917, 8.

Jenkins's cautionary note: Jenkins, *Facing the Hindenburg Line*, 5.

"*He is 28*": Spanier and Trogdon, *Letters*, 54–55.

"*all the dope*": Ibid.

"*In truth*": Ibid., 56.

"*I hit it lucky*": Leicester Hemingway, *My Brother, Ernest Hemingway* (New York: World Publishing, 1961), 45.

Chapter 5: A Lack of Vices

"*rotten looking copy*": Theodore Brumback, "With Hemingway Before 'A Farewell to Arms,'" *Kansas City Star*, December 6, 1936, 1C.

"*Germans tried*": "Ted Brumback Under Fire," *Kansas City Star*, August 26, 1917, 6A.

"*disqualified*": "Brumback Home from France," *Kansas City Star*, November 17, 1917, 1, probably written by Hemingway.

"*Craonne sector*": "Ted Brumback Under Fire."

"*On an ordinary night*": "Fear the Aerial Bomb," *Kansas City Times*, November 23, 1917.

"*Most of the towns I have passed*": Ibid.

"*Two calls were received*": "City Doctors May Quit," *Kansas City Star*, November 5, 1917, 4.

"*may wait till spring*": Spanier and Trogdon, *Letters*, 59.

"*greatest fighters*": Ibid.

"*Canadians are great prowlers*": "Fritz Is Not a Sportsman," *Kansas City Star*, November 4, 1917, 17C.

"inspiring enough": "How He Won His Cross," *Kansas City Star*, December 26, 1917, 3.

"would have been bloody": "Swope Littered by 'Dead,'" *Kansas City Star*, November 14, 1917, 2.

"very thrilling": Spanier and Trogdon, *Letters*, 60.

"He is preserved": Fenton, *Apprenticeship*, 39.

"Moise himself": Moise to George Bye, forwarded to Fenton, May 23, 1952, Beinecke.

"at least ten": Hemingway to Fenton, July 29, 1952, Baker, *Selected Letters*, 774.

"It sort of irks me": Moffett to Fenton, April 27, 1952, Beinecke.

"I knew Moise": Baker, *Selected Letters*, 774.

"Lionel Moise": Item 553, EH Collection. Quoted in full in Baker, *A Life Story*, 35, and Griffin, *Along with Youth*, 42, and elsewhere.

"There was a group of girls": Kenneth Rexroth, *An Autobiographical Novel* (Revised and expanded edition, New York: New Directions, 1991), 137–38.

"I havnt seen a girl": Spanier and Trogdon, *Letters*, 64.

Chapter 6: The "Great Litterateur"

"The man from Chicago": "Wit and Humor as Expounded in Chicago," *Kansas City Star*, November 12, 1917, 16.

Hamsun delivered: "A Street Car Conductor Who Became a Literary Lion," *Kansas City Star*, November 11, 1917, 1C.

One of those episodes: "Police Kill Two in Chase," *Kansas City Times*, November 19, 1917, 1. I first explored the connection between this news story and Hemingway's later vignette in a paper at the 2008 Hemingway Society international conference in Kansas City, which was subsequently expanded and published in *War + Ink*. See also Cohen, *Hemingway's Laboratory*, 162–64.

"I met 'Cap' Gargotta": "Death Breaks Up a Gang," *Kansas City Star*, November 19, 1917, 3.

a compact vignette: Some early critics and other readers, probably led by Fenton, who was misled by *Star* police reporter William Moorhead, have wanted to identify a second vignette, Chapter XV in *In Our Time* ("They hanged Sam Cardinella . . ."), as a Kansas City story. A letter from Hemingway to his father in April 1921 dispels that notion. Hemingway, living in Chicago at the time, walked by the county jail, he said, as a crowd awaited the hanging of Cardinella and two others: Spanier and Trogdon, *Letters*, 280.

The story involved: "Morrow Alford wore suspenders," Item 581, EH Collection.

"Newspaper stories": "Wooed Better as Thief," *Kansas City Star*, November 11, 1917, 12A.

"wouldn't soon forget": "Attacked by Thugs," *Kansas City Star*, September 25, 1910. Stephen L. Harris recounts the newsroom scene in *The Star Maker*, unpublished manuscript.

"The afternoon edition": Courtney Ryley Cooper, "Star Man," *Saturday Evening Post*, December 19, 1936, 23, 56–58.

He told his parents: Spanier and Trogdon, *Letters*, 61–62.

Chapter 7: A Suicide, a Flea, a Vile Place

"Numerous complaints": "U.S. Asks a Cleanup," *Kansas City Star*, December 4, 1917, 1.

"Persons like you": "Beasley's Fine Will Stick," *Kansas City Times*, December 1, 1917, 3.

Secretary Baker in Washington: "Put It Up to Kansas City," *Kansas City Times*, December 8, 1917, 1.

"twenty-one physicians": "Admit a Drug Mart Here," *Kansas City Times*, December 1, 1917, 1.

Doc Kling: Item 471 ("He was quite thin and blonde"), EH Collection.

describes a similar blue: Item 668, EH Collection.

"rotten, immoral": "Tells About Drug Curse," *Kansas City Times*, February 1, 1918, 1.

"a vice-tight lid": "Face an Army Ban Here," *Kansas City Star*, November 8, 1.

"A few minutes after": "A Note Hints at Suicide," *Kansas City Times*, December 5, 1917, 1.

"The suicide note": Spanier and Trogdon, *Letters*, 69.

"Just when a new information": "Bowman Still Avoids Jail," *Kansas City Star*, December 5, 1917, 3.

mature Hemingway whispers: "Kerensky the Fighting Flea," *Kansas City Star*, December 16, 1917, 3C.

"When the gong sounds": "Goat Slate Waits on Tom," *Kansas City Star*, December 8, 1917, 5.

Jefferson Hotel: "Ranson Saves Jefferson," *Kansas City Star*, February 5, 1918, 1.

"Close the Jefferson Hotel": Ibid.

"I can tell mayors": Spanier and Trogdon, *Letters*, 79.

"nice big room": Ibid., 68.

"distinguish chianti": Ibid., 79.

"They are regulation": Ibid., 68–69.

"three special cars": Ibid., 70.

"The major and minor tragedies": "Where the 'Nut Stuff' Pays," *Kansas City Star*, December 16, 1917, 1B.

"I do not doubt": Edgar to Fenton, April 13, 1952, Beinecke.

Hemingway apologized: Spanier and Trogdon, *Letters*, 70.

Chapter 8: The Ambulance Run

"The General Hospital": "War Hits General Hospital," *Kansas City Star*, December 6, 1917, 2.

in a unpublished sketch: Item 241, EH Collection.

dropping the ball: "Pass Buck on Smallpox," *Kansas City Star*, January 2, 1918, 2.

"new and more stringent": "Board Has a New Problem," *Kansas City Star*, January 26, 1918, 1.

"We are making": Spanier and Trogdon, *Letters*, 84.

"arrogant and inefficient": Julian Capers Jr. to Louis Henry Cohn, March 18, 1930. Louis Henry and Marguerite Cohn Ernest Hemingway Collection, University of Delaware Library, Newark, DE.

"While the chauffeur": "Throng at Smallpox Case," *Kansas City Star*, February 18, 1918, 3.

"things have been leaving": "Begin a Health Shakeup," *Kansas City Star*, January 26, 1918, 1.

"Negro who refuses": Bruccoli, *Ernest Hemingway: Cub Reporter*, 27.

Chapter 9: Crime and Punishment

By 8:30 on a Friday night: This account is based on several news stories, beginning on January 14, 1918, including "Fiend Slays Four," *Kansas City Star*, January 16, 1918, 1. I previously explored this crime and the literary discussion that follows in somewhat different form in

"Hemingway in Kansas City: The True Dope on Violence and Creative Sources in a Vile and Lively Place," in *War +Ink*, 1–13.

"A man is born": "Russian Novel Gives Psychology of the Funston Murders," *Kansas City Star*, January 20, 1918, 1B.

"How can a man": *A Moveable Feast*, 137.

"Miss Stein": Fenton, *Apprenticeship*, 158.

Another running story: "Set Over Kreiser Case," *Kansas City Star*, January 14, 1918, 2.

"It was in the first place": "Henry James and the War," *Kansas City Star*, January 2, 1918, 16.

"There were many words": *A Farewell to Arms*, The Hemingway Library Edition, 161.

"enlist together": Spanier and Trogdon, *Letters*, 71.

The phone rang: Ibid., 78.

"There is going": Ibid., 77.

A tractor show: Ibid., 83.

"classy acts": "Prepare for 1919 Show," *Kansas City Star*, February 15, 1918, 3.

"met the fair one": Spanier and Trogdon, *Letters*, 80–82.

"Miss Marsh no kidding": Ibid., 105.

"It took me forty-eight years": Dale Wilson, "Hemingway in Kansas City," *Fitzgerald-Hemingway Annual*, 1976, 216.

"one of my best pals": Spanier and Trogdon, *Letters*, 80–81.

"bristled at injustice": Wilson, "Hemingway in Kansas City," 213–214.

witnessed Leo Fitzpatrick: Marcel Wallenstein, ". . . Adding to His Image as a Tough Guy," *Kansas City Star*, July 28, 1974, G1.

"certain timidity": Wilson, "Hemingway in Kansas City," 215.

"very aggressive": Edgar to Fenton, April 13, 1952, Beinecke.

"can be vitriolic": Edgar to Fenton, March 26, 1952, Beinecke.

"abit to the wild": Spanier and Trogdon, *Letters*, 79.

"Ma Hemingstein's" cookies: Spanier and Trogdon, *Letters*, 83–84.

Chapter 10: The War Beckons

"most frightful bombardment": "Ted Brumback Under Fire," *Kansas City Star*, August 26, 1917, 6.

The story begins: This summary first appeared in somewhat different form in Paul, "'Drive,' He Said," *The Hemingway Review*, 27, no. 1 (Fall 2007): 21–38.

Brumback is sleeping: "Racing with Hun's Shells," *Kansas City Star*, February 10, 1918, 18D.

"not much as a house": Ibid.

four men to serve: "Red Cross Calls Men," *Kansas City Star*, February 22, 1918, 13.

"He learned that": Sanford, *At the Hemingways*, 157.

"I enlisted for immediate service": Spanier and Trogdon, *Letters*, 87.

Hemingway's application to join: Capers to Hemingway, February 23, 1927, EH Collection.

Capers demurred: Capers to Hemingway, April 8, 1927, EH Collection.

"We are panning the hide": Spanier and Trogdon, *Letters*, 85.

doctors were unable to order: "Near Death, Await X-Ray," *Kansas City Star*, February 16, 1918, 2.

One Star story, probably: "Only a Paper 'Saving?'" *Kansas City Star*, February 20, 1918, 2.

"unbelievably rotten": Spanier and Trogdon, *Letters*, 84.

By the end of April: "Health Shakeup to Begin," *Kansas City Star*, April 25, 1918.

"doctors with open offices": "Tells About Drug Curse," *Kansas City Times*, February 1, 1918, 1.

"shocking conditions": "The Rotten Alliance," *Kansas City Star*, February 1, 1918, 18.

drug trafficking: "Record Drug Sales Here," *Kansas City Star*, February 1, 1918, 1.

John L. Sullivan: "Knocked Out 200 Men," *Kansas City Star*, February 2, 1918, 1.

"He also sought": Moorhead, *Police Reporter*, jacket cover flap.

"There were many strikers": Moorhead, *Police Reporter*, 174.

"Hemingway didn't participate": Mel Foor, "Remembering Hemingway's Kansas City Days," *Kansas City Star*, July 21, 1968, D1–2.

A laundry guard riding: "Slay a Laundry Guard," *Kansas City Star*, March 13, 1918, 1. Probably written at least in part by Hemingway.

A general strike: Bill Onasch, "The Streetcar Strikes of 1917–18," Accessed July 25, 2016: www.kclabor.org/streetcar_strikes_of_1917.htm.

he bought Coca-Colas: Spanier and Trogdon, *Letters*, 90.

"Grover Cleveland may not": "'Alec' Left with Cubs," *Kansas City Star*, March 13, 1918, 12.

"The fellows all agreed": Spanier and Trogdon, *Letters*, 85.

"celebrated feast": T. Norman Williams to Hemingway, May 8, 1918, EH Collection.

"soothed my burning brow": T. Norman Williams to Hemingway, December 5, 1919, EH Collection.

Chapter 11: "Snap and Wallop"

"It is these men": Theodore Roosevelt, "From a Father's Heart," *Kansas City Star*, April 2, 1918, 1.

Hemingway listed five: "Six Men Become Tankers," *Kansas City Star*, April 17, 1918, 7.

Thirty-eight men were accepted: "Big Day for Navy Drive," *Kansas City Star*, April 17, 1918, 6.

the navy ordered: "Navy Desk Jobs to Go," *Kansas City Star*, April 18, 1918, 17.

"Four men stood outside": "Would 'Treat 'Em Rough,'" *Kansas City Star*, April 18, 1918, 4.

"Have you ever had": "Dare Devil Joins Tanks," *Kansas City Star*, April 21, 1918, 3A.

"Ernest was a boy": Haskell to Fenton, February 29, 1952, Beinecke.

In mid-April, two weeks: Spanier and Trogdon, *Letters*, 92–94.

"enthusiastic prophecies": Fenton, *Apprenticeship*, 46.

"wholly implicit": Ibid.

The piece was short: "Mix War, Art and Dancing," *Kansas City Star*, April 21, 1918, 1.

Hemingway learned much: From a talk by H. R. Stoneback, July 19, 2016, at the XVIIth Biennial International Hemingway Society Conference, Oak Park, Illinois.

"Lieutenant Roselli said": "'Italy in Fearful State,'" *Kansas City Star*, April 2, 1918, 2.

Nick Adams eventually told: "A Way You'll Never Be," *Complete Short Stories*, 311.

Chapter 12: "You See Things"

"Hemingway was delirious": Theodore Brumback, "With Hemingway Before 'A Farewell to Arms,'" *Kansas City Star*, December 6, 1936, 1C.

"apple cheeked country boy": Henry Van Brunt to Fenton, March 4, 1952, Beinecke.

"We recall": Henry J. Haskell to Fenton, February 29, 1959, Beinecke.

"Ernie, as I knew him": Russel Crouse to Fenton, February 8, 1952, Beinecke.

"the trick of credibility": Reynolds, *The Young Hemingway*, 61.

Clyde Roberts used to tell: William L. Hathaway, e-mail to the author, July 21, 1999.

"Don't let anyone": Fenton, *Apprenticeship*, 47.

"most entertaining soul": Bill Horne to Fenton, April 10, 1952, Beinecke.

"popular and noticeable": "Missouri Notes," *Kansas City Star*, August 3, 1918, 12.

"glowing personality": Roy Dickey to Fenton, May 3, 1952, Beinecke.

"plain damn fool": T. Norman Williams to Hemingway, May 8, 1918, EH Collection.

"Your honors shall be": Ibid.

Moffett recognized that: Elizabeth Moffett to Fenton, April 27, 1952, Beinecke.

promised them a keepsake: Ibid.

"I havnt seen a girl": Spanier and Trogdon, *Letters*, 64.

"He was feeling very grown-up": Sanford, *At the Hemingways*, 156.

"congenial with people": Ibid.

"feeling rather blue": Brumback to Hemingway, May 4, 1918, EH Collection.

"You could rely": Charles H. Hopkins to Clarence Hemingway, July 22, 1918, Manuscripts Department, Lilly Library, Indiana University, Bloomington, Indiana.

At the last train depot: Sanford, *At the Hemingways*, 158–59. Marcelline's version incorrectly implies the railroad stop was in Canada. Her chronology also is suspect, including her statement that Hemingway left New York for Europe on May 28, which is off by five days.

Red Cross telegram: Clarence Hemingway to Ernest, May 7, 1918, EH Collection.

another telegram: Clarence Hemingway to Ernest, May 8, 1918, EH Collection.

"tried eleven times": "Go Together to the Front," *Kansas City Star*, May 13, 1918, 4.

"Libber of Goddesty": Spanier and Trogdon, *Letters*, 98.

Hemingway's letter also itemized: Spanier and Trogdon, *Letters*, 97.

To Dale Wilson: Ibid., 105.

"relieve our minds": Clarence Hemingway to Ernest Hemingway, May 18, 1918, EH Collection.

Just kidding: Spanier and Trogdon, *Letters*, 102.

"Where in Sam Hill": Carl Edgar to Ernest Hemingway, June 18, 1918, EH Collection.

"I felt lonesome": Spanier and Trogdon, *Letters*, 101.

"Anything you want": Ibid., 106.

"lonesome as hell": Ibid., 104.

As so often happened: Florczyk, *Hemingway, the Red Cross*, 33–34.

"rottenest ship": Spanier and Trogdon, *Letters*, 107.

"biggest and best looking": Bill Horne, undated letter to Sue Ellen Farmer, William Horne-Ernest Hemingway Papers, Newberry Library, Chicago (hereafter cited as Horne-Hemingway Papers).

passage was rather dull: Brumback, "With Hemingway."

"The monotony": Ibid

bouts of seasickness: Spanier and Trogdon, *Letters*, 107–8.

"phosphorescent waves": Ibid., 108.

Hemingway also recycled: "Night Before Landing," *The Nick Adams Stories*, 138.

"Drawers of boys' letters": *Complete Poems*, 51.

In Bordeaux: Bill Horne interview by Virginia Kleitz Moseley, "The Hemingway I Remember," *Princeton Alumni Weekly*, November 5, 1979, Horne-Hemingway Papers.

night train for Paris: Ibid.

expert at the language: Spanier and Trogdon, *Letters*, 110.

"The people accept": Ibid.

admirably journalistic job: Florczyk, *Hemingway, the Red Cross*, 40.

eager for a thrill: Brumback, "With Hemingway."

Chapter 13: At the Piave

"We carried them in": "Wounded on Italy Front," Hemingway's postcard from Milan in early June was quoted in the *Kansas City Star*, July 14, 1918, 5A.

"After we had searched": "A Natural History of the Dead," *Complete Short Stories*, 336. Also see Luca Gandolfi, "The Outskirts of Literature:

Uncovering the Munitions Factory in 'A Natural History of the Dead.'" *The Hemingway Review* 19, no. 2 (Spring 2000): 105–7.

"I recall one or two of us": "A Natural History of the Dead," *Complete Short Stories*, 337.

Hemingway, according to: Smith, *Reader's Guide*, 231–39.

"wonderful time": "Wounded on Italy Front," *Kansas City Star*, July 14, 1918, 5A.

Austrians were shelling the town: Brumback, "With Hemingway."

The Section 4 recruits: Ibid.

Hemingway returned with an Austrian handgun: Photograph and caption from the Bill Horne scrapbook. Horne-Hemingway Papers. Other photographs of the souvenir collectors, including one published in this book, are in the Hemingway and Milford Baker Correspondence, Rare Books and Special Collections, Firestone Library, Princeton University, Princeton, New Jersey. See also letter to Ruth Morrison ("my captured Austrian officers automatic pistol"), Spanier and Trogdon, *Letters*, 113.

"cover our sector a little east": Bill Horne interview by Virginia Kleitz Moseley, "The Hemingway I Remember," *Princeton Alumni Weekly*, November 5, 1979, Horne-Hemingway Papers.

In another postcard: Quoted in "Wounded on Italy Front," *Kansas City Star*, July 14, 1918, 5A.

Three Sisters Saloon: Bill Horne, undated letter to Sue Ellen Farmer, Horne-Hemingway Papers.

one-hundred-mile offensive: "Blow at Italy Fails?" *Kansas City Star*, June 16, 1918, 1A.

"fed up": Brumback, "With Hemingway."

"rudimentary base": Florczyk, *Hemingway, the Red Cross*, 67.

Lt. Edward McKey: Reynolds, *Hemingway's First War*, 147–48.

"ugly sight": Capt. Robert W. Bates, Red Cross commanding officer, quoted in Florczyk, *Hemingway, the Red Cross*, 68.

it had four rooms: Spanier and Trogdon, *Letters*, 113.

Hemingway urged Morrison: Ibid.

two or three cents: Brumback, "With Hemingway."

"his smiling face": Brumback to Clarence and Grace Hall Hemingway, July 14, 1918, in Spanier and Trogdon, *Letters*, 115.

"I watched a clever Italian": Ibid.

at Roncade, Hemingway heard: Mamoli Zorzi and Moriani, *In Venice*, 50. See also *Across the River and into the Trees*, 53.

"The concussion of the explosion": Brumback to Clarence and Grace Hall Hemingway, in Spanier and Trogdon, *Letters*, 115–16. Brumback's letter was published in the Oak Park newspaper, *Oak Leaves*, on August 10, 1918, and in the *Kansas City Star* the next day.

moonless night: Baker, *A Life Story*, 44.

Baker attributed: Baker, *A Life Story*, endnote, 571. See Hemingway to his family, August 18, 1918, in Spanier and Trogdon, *Letters*, 130–33.

"His legs felt": Baker, *A Life Story*, 45.

Florczyk makes a detailed: Florczyk, *Hemingway, the Red Cross*, 70–97.

In late July: W. R. Castle Jr. to C. E. Hemingway, July 20, 1918, EH Collection. Hemingway's mother transcribed the letter and forwarded it to him in Milan.

"had been commended": Red Cross bulletin, quoted in Florczyk, *Hemingway, the Red Cross*, 81.

"Courage and coolness": *Report of the Department of Military Affairs, January 1918 to February 1919* (Rome: Commission of the American Red Cross), 24.

"twisted a tourniquet": "A Veteran Visits the Old Front," *Dateline: Toronto*, 176.

"Italian I had with me": Spanier and Trogdon, *Letters*, 131.

What remains essential: "Now I Lay Me," in *Complete Short Stories*, 276.

to the mayor's house: Mamoli Zorzi and Moriani, *In Venice*, 50.

"When it came": Spanier and Trogdon, *Letters*, 131.

"Don't go back to visit": "A Veteran Visits the Old Front," *Dateline: Toronto*, 176–80.

"misleading thesis": Reynolds, *Hemingway's First War*, 283.

his supposed heroism: Florczyk, *Hemingway, the Red Cross*, 88, 95–97.

adulation for the sacrifice: Henry S. Villard, "In a World War I Hospital with Hemingway," *Horizon*, August 1918, 93. Villard's account later appeared in a different version in Villard and Nagel, *Hemingway in Love and War*.

particularly disgusted: quoted in Florczyk, *Hemingway, the Red Cross*, 85.

"impossible to distinguish": Celia Kingsbury, "A Way It Never Was," in Paul, Sinclair, and Trout, eds., *War + Ink*, 150–51.

crude line drawing: Spanier and Trogdon, *Letters*, 119.

Chapter 14: Lies and Disillusionment

"I wouldn't say": Spanier and Trogdon, *Letters*, 130. Quoted in "A Note on Ernest Hemingway's Great Transformation in War," *Kansas City Times*, July 7, 1936, 14.

"His injury at Fossalta": Donaldson, *By Force of Will*, 126.

"When you go to war": *Men at War*, xii.

"braggart warrior": Donaldson, *By Force of Will*, 139–43.

"hasty, impulsive": Quoted in Villard, "In a World War I Hospital," 92. The quote appears in slightly different form in "Red Cross Driver in Italy," Villard's opening chapter in Villard and Nagel, *Hemingway in Love and War*, 41.

No one should worry: Spanier and Trogdon, *Letters*, 147.

"Does all that sound like": Ibid., 148.

"only feebly": Charles Hopkins to Clarence Hemingway, July 22, 1918, Manuscripts Department, Lilly Library, Indiana University, Bloomington, Indiana.

Tubby Williams: T. Norman Williams to Clarence and Grace Hall Hemingway, July 20, 1918, EH Collection. Anyone looking to explore Hemingway's friendship with Tubby could be thrown by the evidence in this letter, which is a copy that Grace Hall Hemingway typed and forwarded to her son; she transcribed the signature as "Hamon Williams."

telegram from the Red Cross: "Wounded on Italy Front," *Kansas City Star*, July 14, 1918, 5A.

"lonesome Jonathan": Postcard to Hemingway from Elizabeth Pratt Brumback, July 14, 1918, EH Collection.

"Your pants and shoe": Ted Brumback to Hemingway, July 19, 1918, EH Collection.

"wheeling chair": Ted Brumback to Hemingway, August 8, 1918, EH Collection.

"sea slugs": "Wild Gastronomic Adventures of a Gourmet," in *Dateline: Toronto*, 371–76.

"Many a night": Ibid.

"one of the finest books": *Men at War*, xvi.

"the Lord ordained": Spanier and Trogdon, *Letters*, 162.

Hemingway portrayed Farrell: "The Ash Heel's Tendon—A Story," in Griffin, *Along with Youth*, 174–80.

"In those days": *Complete Short Stories*, 298.

The critic Harold Bloom: Harold Bloom, *How to Read and Why* (New York: Simon and Schuster, 2000), 47.

Patrick Hemingway: Conversation with the author, April 10, 2016. Also see Item 526 ("It Was Very Hot in Constantinople"), EH Collection.

dens of iniquity: I once attempted to connect the dots between Kansas City and Constantinople in an article based on previously unpublished fragments of the short story's manuscript, which offered unprecedented (for Hemingway) details of Kansas City's Union Station: "Hemingway's Kansas City," *Kansas City Star*, June 27, 1999, 1A. Online: www.kansascity.com/entertainment/arts-culture /article295158/Hemingways-Kansas-CitybrbrBrief-but-telling -early-jottings-reveal-authors-ties-to-town.html.

"The autobiographical story": Meyers, *Hemingway: A Biography*, 50.

fodder for A Farewell to Arms: Reynolds, *Hemingway's First War*, 180.

"the most interesting reading": *Complete Short Stories*, 113.

"did not want to talk": Ibid., 111.

"distaste for everything": Ibid.

"Roarin thru Schio": "There was Ike and Tony and Jaque and me," *Complete Poems*, 18.

"Soldiers pitch": "Champs d'Honneur," *Complete Poems*, 27.

"Desire and": "Killed Piave—July 8—1918," *Complete Poems*, 35.

an intriguing notion: Reynolds, *Hemingway's First War*, 147–49.

"central point": Ibid., 170.

At the typewriter: "Mitrailliatrice," *Complete Poems*, 37.

go to war again: Spanier and Trogdon, *Letters*, 152.

cubist collages: Thomas Strychacz, "*In Our Time*, Out of Season," in *The Cambridge Companion to Ernest Hemingway*, ed. Scott Donaldson (Cambridge: Cambridge University Press, 1996), 60.

"You and me": "Chapter VI," *Complete Short Stories*, 105. This and the other vignettes also appear in Hemingway's first American story collection, *In Our Time*, and in *The Nick Adams Stories*.

Coda

"lay under a Ford": "Back to His First Field," *Kansas City Times*, November 26, 1940, 1.

BIBLIOGRAPHY

Baker, Carlos. *Ernest Hemingway: A Life Story.* New York: Scribner, 1969. Paperback, Collier Books, 1988.

———, ed. *Ernest Hemingway: Selected Letters, 1917–1961.* New York: Charles Scribner's Sons, 1981.

———. *Hemingway: The Writer as Artist.* Princeton, NJ: Princeton University Press, 1962.

Beegel, Susan F., ed. *Hemingway's Neglected Short Fiction: New Perspectives.* Ann Arbor: UMI Research Press, 1989.

Brasch, James D., and Joseph Sigman. *Hemingway's Library: A Composite Record.* New York: Garland, 1981. Accessible online at the Kennedy Library: www.jfklibrary.org/Research/The-Ernest-Hemingway -Collection/~/media/C107EFE32F9C446A8A30B7C46C4B035F.pdf.

Bruccoli, Matthew J., ed. *Ernest Hemingway: Cub Reporter.* Pittsburgh: University of Pittsburgh Press, 1970.

Cohen, Milton A. *Hemingway's Laboratory: The Paris in our time.* Tuscaloosa: University of Alabama Press, 2005.

Davis, Clyde Brion. *"The Great American Novel --".* New York: Farrar and Rinehart, 1938.

Donaldson, Scott. *By Force of Will: The Life and Art of Ernest Hemingway.* New York: Viking, 1977.

———, ed. *The Cambridge Companion to Ernest Hemingway.* New York: Cambridge University Press, 1996.

Elder, Robert K., Aaron Vetch, and Mark Cirino. *Hidden Hemingway: Inside the Ernest Hemingway Archives of Oak Park.* Kent, OH: Kent State University Press, 2016.

Federspiel, Michael R. *Picturing Hemingway's Michigan*. Detroit: Wayne State University Press/Painted Turtle, 2010.

Fenton, Charles A. *The Apprenticeship of Ernest Hemingway: The Early Years*. New York: Farrar, Straus and Young, 1954.

Florczyk, Steven. *Hemingway, the Red Cross, and the Great War*. Kent, OH: Kent State University Press, 2014.

Fussell, Paul. *The Great War and Modern Memory*. New York: Oxford University Press, 1975.

Garnett, E. B. *Life on The Star as I Lived It*. Unpublished manuscript and drafts, located in the *Kansas City Star* archives.

Garwood, Darrell. *Crossroads of America: The Story of Kansas City*. New York: W. W. Norton, 1948.

Gladden, Norman. *Across the Piave: A Personal Account of the British Forces in Italy, 1917–1919*. London: Imperial War Museum/Her Majesty's Stationery Office, 1971.

Griffin, Peter. *Along with Youth: Hemingway, the Early Years*. New York: Oxford University Press, 1985.

Hanneman, Audre. *Ernest Hemingway: A Comprehensive Bibliography*. Princeton, NJ: Princeton University Press, 1967.

———. *Supplement to Ernest Hemingway: A Comprehensive Bibliography*. Princeton, NJ: Princeton University Press, 1975.

Hansen, Arlen J. *Gentlemen Volunteers: The Story of the American Ambulance Drivers in the Great War*. New York: Arcade, 1996.

Harris, Stephen L. *The Star Maker*. Unpublished manuscript. Based on interviews conducted with former *Kansas City Star* staffers, circa 1974–1976.

Haskell, Harry. *Boss-Busters & Sin Hounds: Kansas City and Its* Star. Columbia: University of Missouri Press, 2007.

Hemingway, Alfred T. *How to Make Good; or Winning Your Largest Success*. Kansas City, MO: Personal Proficiency Bureau/Franklin Hudson, 1915.

Hemingway, Ernest. *Across the River and into the Trees*. New York: Charles Scribner's Sons, 1950.

———. *Byline: Ernest Hemingway*. Edited by William White. New York: Charles Scribner's Sons, 1967.

———. *Complete Poems*. Edited by Nicholas Gerogiannis. Revised edition. Lincoln: University of Nebraska Press, 1992.

———. *The Complete Short Stories of Ernest Hemingway: The Finca Vigia Edition*. New York: Charles Scribner's Sons, 1987.

———. *Dateline: Toronto*. Edited by William White. New York: Charles Scribner's Sons, 1985.

———. *A Farewell to Arms*. New York: Charles Scribner's Sons, 1929. Paperback, Scribner, 1969. The Hemingway Library Edition, including drafts and other material, Scribner, 2012.

———. *Death in the Afternoon*. New York: Charles Scribner's Sons, 1932. Paperback, Scribner, 1996.

———. *In Our Time*. New York: Charles Scribner's Sons, 1925. Paperback, Scribner, 1996.

———, ed. *Men at War*. New York: Crown, 1942. Reprint, Wings Books, 1992.

———. *A Moveable Feast*. New York: Charles Scribner's Sons, 1964. Paperback, Scribner, 1998. Restored Edition, edited by Seán Hemingway, New York: 2009.

———. *The Nick Adams Stories*. New York: Charles Scribner's Sons, 1972.

———. *The Sun Also Rises*. New York: Charles Scribner's Sons, 1926. Hemingway Library Edition, edited by Seán Hemingway, Scribner, 2014.

Jenkins, Burris A. *Facing the Hindenburg Line*. New York: Fleming H. Revell, 1917.

Larsen, Lawrence H., and Nancy J. Hulston. *Pendergast!* Columbia: University of Missouri Press, 1997.

Mamoli Zorzi, Rosella, and Gianni Moriani. *In Venice and in the Veneto with Ernest Hemingway*. Venice: Dipartimento di Studi Linguistici e Culturali Compariti of the University Ca' Foscari of Venice and Venice International University, 2011.

Maziarka, Cynthia, and Donald Vogel Jr. *Hemingway at Oak Park High: The High School Writings of Ernest Hemingway, 1916-1917*. Oak Park, IL: Oak Park and River Forest High School, 1993.

Mellow, James R. *Hemingway: A Life Without Consequences*. Paperback, Cambridge, MA: Perseus, 1992.

Meyers, Jeffrey. *Hemingway: A Biography*. New York: Harper and Row, 1985.

Miller, Madelaine Hemingway. *Ernie: Hemingway's Sister "Sunny" Remembers*. New York: Crown, 1975.

Moorhead, William B. (Bill). *Police Reporter*. Kansas City, MO: Privately published, 1955.

Nagel, James, ed. *Ernest Hemingway: The Oak Park Legacy*. Tuscaloosa: University of Alabama Press, 1996.

Paul, Steve, Gail Sinclair, and Steven Trout, eds. *War + Ink: New Perspectives on Ernest Hemingway's Early Life and Writings*. Kent, OH: Kent State University Press, 2014.

Reddig, William M. *Tom's Town: Kansas City and the Pendergast Legend*. Paperback, Columbia: University of Missouri Press, 1996.

Reynolds, Michael. *Hemingway's First War: The Making of "A Farewell to Arms."* Princeton, NJ: Princeton University Press, 1976. Reprinted, New York and Oxford: Basil Blackwell, 1987.

———. *The Young Hemingway*. New York: Basil Blackwell, 1986. Reprinted, New York: W. W. Norton, 1998.

Sandison, David. *Ernest Hemingway: An Illustrated Biography*. Chicago: Chicago Review Press, 1999.

Sanford, Marcelline Hemingway. *At the Hemingways: With Fifty Years of Correspondence Between Ernest and Marcelline Hemingway*. Centennial Edition, Moscow: University of Idaho Press. 1999.

Shippey, Lee. *The Luckiest Man Alive*. Los Angeles: Westernlore, 1959.

Smith, Paul. *A Reader's Guide to the Short Stories of Ernest Hemingway*. Boston: G. K. Hall, 1989.

Spanier, Sandra, and Robert W. Trogdon, eds. *The Letters of Ernest Hemingway, Vol. 1: 1907–1922*. Cambridge, UK: Cambridge University Press, 2011.

Stout, Ralph, ed. *Roosevelt in The Kansas City Star: War-Time Editorials by Theodore Roosevelt*. Boston: Houghton Mifflin, 1921.

Villard, Henry S., and James Nagel. *Hemingway in Love and War: The Lost Diary of Agnes von Kurowsky*. New York: Hyperion, 1996.

CREDITS

In using material by Ernest Hemingway, numerous correspondents, and others, I have attempted to gain permission from copyright holders. Many of those sources quoted in this book are long deceased, and in most cases, especially those involving lesser-known correspondents, heirs could not be found. I am grateful for all the archivists and others who gave permission to use material in this book. Many of those people and collections are identified in the acknowledgments. If an error or omission has occurred, please bring it to the attention of the publisher.

Image credits appear with each photograph.

I owe many thanks to the Ernest Hemingway Society and Foundation, the Hemingway family, Simon & Schuster, and others for use of quotations from certain materials, including the following.

Across the River and into the Trees by Ernest Hemingway: Reprinted with permission of Scribner, a division of Simon & Schuster, Inc. Copyright © 1950 by Ernest Hemingway. Copyright renewed 1978 by Mary Hemingway.

From *The Complete Short Stories of Ernest Hemingway, The Finca Vigia Edition*: "A Way You'll Never Be" and "God Rest You Merry, Gentlemen," copyright © 1933 by Charles Scribner's Sons. Copyright renewed © 1961 by Mary Hemingway. "Now I Lay Me," copyright © 1927 by Charles Scribner's Sons. Copyright renewed

INDEX

Page numbers in italics refer to images.